IMAGES
of America

NAPA VALLEY
FARMING

BEATRICE LUHMANN AND FARM MANAGER GEORGE NICHOL. Friend Marilyn Grover remembers, "Beatrice worked on her farm right up until her death at 85. She was very chipper, high spirited. I loved to take Beatrice for a drive anywhere around the Valley; she knew everyone, could point out much of what you were looking at. In a family plot at Tulocay there is Henry and Beatrice, then two brothers, their two sons, and George Nichols there on the end in the same plot. Nichols had done the chores, feeding chickens, always pushing a broom around. He had a railroad pension from the East, and lived at a little place on their farm."

History is the witness that testifies to the passing of time; it illumines reality, vitalizes memory, provides guidance in daily life and brings us tidings of antiquity.

—Cicero, *Pro Publio Sestio*

ON THE COVER: This photograph was taken August 1947 in the Grande/Rossi pear orchards on Silverado Trail, two days after Theodore Rossi died. Gathered here to help bring in the harvest are Domenica Rossi, Hazel Hasey, Vena Grande (Dorothy's mother), Antonio Rossi, Rossi's army sergeant Frank Brenkweitz, and his wife Amy Brenkweitz.

IMAGES
of America

NAPA VALLEY
FARMING

Paula Amen Judah and Lauren Coodley
with the Napa County Historical Society

ARCADIA
PUBLISHING

ISBN 978-1-5316-4966-1

Published by Arcadia Publishing
Charleston, South Carolina

Library of Congress Control Number: 2010942412

For all general information, please contact Arcadia Publishing:
Telephone 843-853-2070
Fax 843-853-0044
E-mail sales@arcadiapublishing.com
For customer service and orders:
Toll-Free 1-888-313-2665

Visit us on the Internet at www.arcadiapublishing.com

*To my mother, MaryEllen Simmons,
my son Patrick James Judah,
and my daughter, Amy Bernadette Judah*

—Paula Amen Judah

*To my teacher, JJ Wilson,
and my grandsons Oscar and Diego Vega*

—Lauren Coodley

CONTENTS

ACKNOWLEDGMENTS

The authors heartily thank Laura Chaney, their editor at Arcadia Publishing, who championed this project from the beginning and cheered us on daily. A bow goes to acquisitions editor Coleen Balent and production director David Mandel, who picked up the reins in the closing phases of publication. We were fortunate also to have the support of the Napa County Historical Society and executive director Kristie Sheppard, who spent hours retrieving, organizing, and scanning images from the organization's archives. We appreciate, as well, her publication committee for ascertaining the historical accuracy of each caption. Special admiration goes to Peggy Aaron, intrepid and enthusiastic sleuth, whose knowledge of local history, unique relationships with community elders, and dedication to preserving their stories, resulted in many of the fine images held within these pages.

From the moment Stephanie Grohs brought her to David Wheatley's prune farm, Lauren began to see the valley in a new way; Stephanie continued to provide a wealth of crucial research for this book and a holistic grasp of local histories. Lauren thanks Pat Alexander for sharing images from her brilliant book on Yountville and new Arcadia author Sharon McGriff Payne for introducing her to Delilah Beasley's research. Marc Babin, who once delivered malfatti to the Connolly sisters, kept the computer humming. Last, thanks to historian Lauren Ellsworth, whose enthusiasm and organizational skills have literally made this project possible and to son Nils McCune for joining the ongoing struggle of peoples everywhere to grow their own food.

Paula thanks Laure Latham, author of *A Frog Mom in California,* for her interview notes and beautiful photographs; Pacific Union College librarian Gilberto Abella for the hours he spent locating images of early farming there, which add to the vigor of this book; and Julie Lee, who helped in that effort. Warmest thanks go to husband Mark Schmitt, who never complained about the hours of neglect while she was researching and writing. Paula credits Napa teachers Ed Soloman and Bernard O'Haire for sparking her young interest in history. Last, a bow to beloved stepfather George Simmons, whose spirit and love of growing things buoyed her throughout this project.

Paula and Lauren thank each other for what seems a lifetime of sharing friendship and discovering together the joy of uncovering local history. Though wild women may get the blues, if they are blessed to grow older together, they may find sustenance in the stories, the poems, the recipes, and the memories of others.

INTRODUCTION

Home is the site of natural epiphanies: the sky and the earth touch in a certain way, horizons are vast or impeded, light has a certain quality of radiance, rain comes in steady drizzles or drenching downpours . . . local history puts us in touch with the embodied child and the conjuring writer. It brings us to the common rural edge where village, region, and world meet.

—Joseph Amato, *Rethinking Home*

Once upon a time, indigenous peoples came over the land bridge to North America. They migrated, about 30,000 years ago, to the fertile valley known as Napa. These original inhabitants of Napa's valley drew nourishment from the plants that were growing here, within the hunter-gatherer lifestyle characteristic of all original peoples. The first chapter of this book presents the plants that sustained them, the tools and baskets they created to prepare and store the plants, and some ideas of how they were cooked and cultivated.

In 1821, the lives of indigenous peoples changed dramatically when the Mexican government built what would be the last mission in Sonoma. In order to obtain this land, Mariano Vallejo led the Mexican army as it dislocated the indigenous and apportioned the hills and the valley east of Sonoma to his friends, a group who called themselves Californios. These men prospered, growing citrus fruit, corn, beans, barley, peas, mission grapes, nuts, and wheat.

Under Mexican rule, cattle ranching and wheat growing in California began, offering economic opportunities to Californios while indigenous and landless Mexican peoples remained in a permanent position of servitude on the ranchos. Cattle came to Napa in the 1830s when Nasario Berryessa brought 5,000 head to the area, which he ran between Berryessa and Capay Valleys. American settler George Yount came to the Napa area in 1835 and was given a land grant by Mariano Vallejo. His home became a gathering place for American emigrants.

In 1848, at the end of the Mexican American War, America gained much of the territory that was once Mexico, and Californio rights to land ownership ended. American settlers from all parts of the country moved in to claim the land or to buy it. Former gold miner William Thompson traded lumber with Mariano Vallejo. In return, Vallejo gave Thompson a parcel of his land, and Thompson purchased an additional 300 acres. In 1852, Thompson's brother Simpson suggested planting a fruit orchard. Gold seekers weary of a monotonous diet of beef and grain were willing to pay high prices for fresh fruit. Thompson and his brother ordered saplings delivered by boat from the East Coast. They planted some of the first peach and apple trees near Suscol Creek, which they diverted and channeled for irrigation. The second chapter of this book offers images documenting the ways in which the "settlers from south and east" took over this valley. By 1860, Thompson's Gardens were known all over the west and 150,000 peach and apple trees were thriving; also by that year, many newly emancipated African Americans were farming in the Napa Valley.

The images in the third chapter document Napa's agricultural life in the half century from 1880 to 1930. During this period, Rudolph Boysen cultivated the first boysenberry, and Napa pears were characterized by the *San Francisco Chronicle* as "reaching a fine state of perfection." Napans made apple cider, dried grapes into raisins, drove dairy wagons, and shipped eggs to San Francisco. The electric railroad extended from Vallejo to Calistoga, and for a 15¢ round-trip ticket, women could ride the train to work at the cannery in east Napa.

The main employer during the fruit-picking season was the Napa Fruit company which became famous for its "Napa Pack." William Fisher installed a fruit dehydrator on his property near Union Station at Trancas where other fruit growers would bring their stock. In summer, kids' hands and knees were sticky with juice as they picked prunes, earning 15–25¢ a box to buy school clothes. Chapter four features local families working together in their orchards. Here also are agricultural students working in the fields and dairies of Pacific Union College. In Monticello, a small town just east of Napa, the annual springtime cattle roundup began in 1926; by the 1930s, thousands traveled to the event.

Chapters five and six document the last 50 years, as acres of orchards started disappearing. During this period, the Bale Mill in Calistoga became a state historic site where children came to learn about the olden days; the DeHaven prunes and pears were cut down to make way for a mobile home park; the orchards on Oak Knoll, West Lincoln, Redwood Road, Big Ranch Road, Thompson Avenue, Old Sonoma Road, Browns Valley Road, and Mt. Veeder were gradually converted to vineyards, schools, and housing. During these years, the Guiducci and Tanita families picked their last prunes, while the Vu family ventured out to gather pears at the community college, where the last of the orchards of Napa Asylum still bloomed. Author Paula Amen Judah remembers:

> When I started kindergarten at Lincoln School in 1946, Napa was surrounded by orchards and pastures. Fruit and cattle formed the background of my childhood. Back then, a traditional spring outing for our family was "going for a ride." Our dad would begin the journey west, meandering through town toward Browns Valley, eventually entering the narrow road bisecting acres of orchards. I would lean my head out the window, savoring the sight and smell of thousands of fruit blossoms, eyes taking in the sweeping slide show of rows upon rows of blossoming trees: *This bounty was ours.*

Janet Pierson Swan remembers picking prunes in the fall with her sister Diana, near Oak Knoll, testament to the orchards that once blanketed the area. Stewart Duhig writes of his mother canning 200 quarts of fruit a year on their Carneros farm. Like other women, she must have gloried in having a taste of summer in a jar on a cold winter night. Jerry Aaron, Don Judah, and Marshall Jaeger tell stories of picking pears in the 1960s for Mr. Meilink on Redwood Road and prunes for Ed Tanita on Big Ranch Road, where a solitary prune tree still stands.

In the 1990s, the Connolly sisters deeded their farm to the children of Napa. The Ellsworth and McCune children continued to celebrate their birthdays surrounded by pear and walnut trees. Although by 2009 wine grapes accounted for over 99 percent of the county's harvest, Napans still treasure local produce. Jack Tognetti is harvesting and selling his top grade walnuts on Bayview Avenue in Carneros, while Dr. Dinwiddie's peach stand and Dorothy Rossi's egg sign still grace Silverado Trail, and Swede Johnson offers honey for sale by the quart.

Images of Napa's heritage go beyond the photos is this book. We can find them in small orchards and backyards across the city and county: in a half-row of plums on the side of a rural road, in two old sister peach trees behind a house in Fairview Terrace, in a majestic walnut tree spreading shade across a lawn on Imola Avenue. A poem or recipe introduces each chapter, tribute to the ingenuity that produced these experiments in the kitchen, along with the effort it took to record them. Both of these arts provide sustenance—both are ways of responding to the bounty of harvest: by slicing fruit or taking pen to paper. We invite you to read the poems aloud, to try the recipes. We thank you for joining us to honor those who are part of, and making, our history.

ORCHARD
by Hilda "H.D." Doolittle (1886–1961)

These fallen hazel-nuts,
Stripped late of their green sheaths,
Grapes, red-purple,
Their berries
Dripping with wine,
Pomegranates already broken,
And shrunken figs
And quinces untouched,
I bring you as offering.

One

WHAT THE WOODS AND FIELDS ARE MADE OF

20,000 BC–1820

A CALENDAR OF SONNETS
by Helen Hunt Jackson

June

O month whose promise and fulfilment blend,
And burst in one! it seems the earth can store
In all her roomy house no treasure more;
Of all her wealth no farthing have to spend
On fruit, when once this stintless flowering end.
And yet no tiniest flower shall fall before
It hath made ready at its hidden core
Its tithe of seed, which we may count and tend
Till harvest. Joy of blossomed love, for thee
Seems it no fairer thing can yet have birth?
No room is left for deeper ecstasy?
Watch well if seeds grow strong, to scatter free
Germs for thy future summers on the earth.
A joy which is but joy soon comes to dearth.

September

The golden-rod is yellow;
The corn is turning brown;
The trees in apple orchards
With fruit are bending down.

The gentian's bluest fringes
Are curling in the sun;
In dusty pods the milkweed
Its hidden silk has spun.

The sedges flaunt their harvest,
In every meadow nook;
And asters by the brook-side
Make asters in the brook.

From dewy lanes at morning
The grapes' sweet odors rise;
At noon the roads all flutter
With yellow butterflies . . .

SEASONAL ROUND. The seasonal round reflects the indigenous idea of the circle of life. Indigenous people traveled to California over the Asian land bridge in waves beginning more than 10,000 years ago. Once in the area now known as Napa, they developed an intricate knowledge of the plants and animals they considered kin. (Courtesy Vera-Mae Fredrickson and David Peri.)

CALIFORNIA BLACK OAK: *QUERCUS KELLOGGII*; KHOTHI SO (KA HO'TH SHO). ACORN. KHOTHIS (KHO'TISH). Acorns were the most important food crop for the indigenous people; they preferred those of the black oak and the tanbark oak. Men and women collected acorns together and stored them in specially built caches. Women dried, shelled, ground, and leeched them in preparation for cooking. They pounded shelled acorns in a stone mortar made of igneous rock, stored them beside a creek to remove the bitter tannin, and used them in mush, soup, and bread. (Courtesy Lauren Coodley.)

CALIFORNIA BAY: *UMBELLULARIA CALIFORNICA*; CUSE (CHU'SHEY). Indigenous people roasted bay nuts in their shells in hot ashes, ground them into flour, and formed them into small balls or cakes, which they stored for eating later. (Courtesy Lauren Coodley.)

11

BLUE ELDERBERRY: *SAMBUCUS CAERULEA;* **KATE (KAH'TEY).** Ripe elderberries were eaten fresh, or cooked like acorn mush, and also dried for winter use. Violet Parrish Chappell and Vivian Parrish Wilder, Pomo Kashia elders, write, "Wherever our villages were, wherever we picked our food, those places are blessed places . . . We dedicated our trees not to be cut. The trees in the forest are blessed." (Courtesy Lauren Coodley.)

GHOST PINE: *PINUS SABINIANA;* **NAYO (NIGH'YO).** This tree offered nuts, which the people cracked and ate raw or roasted. (Courtesy Lauren Coodley.)

ANGELICA: *ANGELICA TOMENTOSA*; **CIWHEL** (TSEE'WHEL) FLOWER AND **KUPIS** (COO'PIS) ROOT. Indigenous people ate the immature flowers and green shoots raw. They wore root sections to protect against misfortune, rubbed the ground root on their arms for luck, and smoked the root scrapings. (Courtesy Lauren Coodley.)

HAZELNUTS: *CORYLUS CORNUTA VAR. CALIFORNICA*; **MITI SOHOL** (ME TE SHOW'HO). Hazelnuts were dried in their shells and sometimes roasted before eating. (Courtesy Lauren Coodley.)

TOYON: *HETEROMELES ARBUTIFOLIA;* UNU CIWA HOE (OO NOO TSAW'WA HOE). Toyon berries were eaten after baking or roasting them in a basket of hot coals. The berries of the Toyon and Madrone were the last harvest of the year. The elders write, "Everything was from the Creation. That is why we take care of it. That is what the leader did; she taught us to take care of the food, the water . . . It is a blessing to pick food. It is a blessing to roam around." (Courtesy Lauren Coodley.)

MADRONE: *ARBUTUS MENZIESII;* NAPAYOKO (NA PA YO'KO). First inhabitants ate these berries fresh, or parched them by tossing in a basket with hot coals. They made healing infusions from madrone bark and leaves. (Courtesy Lauren Coodley.)

BUCKEYE: *AESCULUS CALIFORNICA*; SUMOTO (SHU MOW'TOW). Indigenous women pounded buckeye nuts, leached them repeatedly in a sand basin and baked them for several hours. They used the nuts in soup or gruel. (Courtesy Lauren Coodley.)

MANZANITA: *ARCTOSTAPHYLOS MANZANITA*; CANO (CHA'NO); MOTA CANO (MO'TA CHA'NO).
Indigenous people ate the berries fresh or dried, made them into a drink similar to apple cider, and ground nuts into flour for cakes. (Courtesy Lauren Coodley.)

MORTARS AND PESTLE. Author Ursula LeGuin, who spent summers in the Napa Valley, writes, "One may listen but all the words of their language are gone, gone utterly. They worked obsidian, and that stays; down there at the edge of the rich man's airport, there was a workshop, and you can pick up plenty of chipped pieces, but no one has found a finished point for years. There is no other trace of them. They owned their valley very lightly, with easy hands. They walked softly here." (Courtesy Stuart Alexander and Napa Valley Museum.)

MORTAR, PESTLE, AND TOOLS. Because the plant world was sacred and central to their lives, indigenous residents developed many methods of plant cultivation and care. They pruned, weeded, and aerated the soil, carefully taking only the plants they needed. When they gathered seeds for pinole, they would cast a few handfuls back to the ground to assure a yield the following season. They pruned shrubs almost to the ground, stimulating regrowth of the long, straight, slender branches needed for tool and basket making, and periodically they burned the landscape to control underbrush and acorn and bulb growth. (Courtesy Stuart Alexander and Napa Valley Museum.)

BASKETS. Women peeled and split stems and twigs to form watertight baskets, interweaving them with lighter-colored stems to create patterns. They adorned the baskets with feathers, clamshells, and beads, used them for cooking and storing food, and for carrying their infants. Baskets represented the center of indigenous social and spiritual lives. (Courtesy of the Napa Valley Museum; photograph by Stuart Alexander.)

Two

SETTLERS FROM SOUTH AND EAST

1821–1880

SOUR CREAM APPLE PIE
by Loraine Geddes
Napa Community Projects, Inc. cookbook, *Cooking Pleasures* (1971)

5-7 apples (according to size)
8 pieces Zwieback
1 cup sour cream
3 eggs
juice from 1 lemon
salt
sugar
butter
1 cup finely chopped walnuts

Roll Zwieback into fine crumbs. Butter 8-inch pie tin. Line pie tin with Zwieback (3/4 inches thick). Peel and core apples and cut into eighths. Partially cook by steaming with butter and a little sugar. To the apples, add 1 cup sour cream, beaten eggs, a little more sugar, the lemon juice, and the salt. Pour mixture into crumb shell and top with nuts.

Bake slowly in 350-degree oven for about 40 minutes. Serve with whipped cream.

DON IGNACIO VALLEJO. Descended from Castilians, Ignacio Vallejo was born in Mexico in 1748 and came to Monterey, California in 1774. He was a soldier, whose son Don Mariano Guadalupe Vallejo followed in his footsteps. (Courtesy Napa County Historical Society.)

GEN. MARIANO VALLEJO. Vallejo grew up at the Monterey Presidio, where his family owned property. He began his military career at the age of 16, proving his loyalty to the Mexican government by attacking some indigenous tribes, at the same time making treaties with others who helped him maintain Mexican rule over his part of California. Vallejo settled in the Sonoma Valley in 1835, awarding land grants to his friends and favorite soldiers. Oranges, lemons, and olive trees grew and bore fruit in his own garden. (Courtesy Napa County Historical Society.)

CAYETANO JUAREZ AND SON. The Juarez family came to California as soldiers in the Spanish colonial army, where Sgt. Cayetano Juarez helped Vallejo found the Sonoma Presidio. But in 1837, when Mexico did not pay its soldiers, Juarez organized a mass desertion of soldiers who planned to ride from Sonoma to Monterey to demand payment. Juarez swam across the Carquinez Straits with his horse. Just short of Monterey, he was captured and sentenced to be shot. Vallejo intervened and ordered Juarez to marry instead and gave him Tulocay Rancho, where eventually Tulocay Cemetery as well as the Napa State Hospital would be located. (Courtesy Napa County Historical Society.)

LAST RESIDENCE OF CAYETANO AND MARIA JUAREZ, SILVERADO TRAIL, 1874. On the ranchos, beans, corn, onions, grapes, barley, oats, and wheat were grown. In this period, wheat was threshed by piling it inside enclosures and driving wild horses around and around at high speeds until it became pulverized. Then workers would repeatedly lift and toss the mass with forks until the wind blew away the straw and chaff, leaving the grain, which they washed, dried, and made ready for milling. Californio women, who typically were pregnant most of their reproductive lives, had responsibility for running the ranchos while the men were away for long periods of time. Maria Juarez had 11 children at Rancho Tulocay. (Courtesy Napa County Historical Society.)

GEORGE YOUNT. The first land grant that Vallejo bestowed was not given to a Californio but to an American George Yount, who had migrated from Missouri to California in 1833. Yount had won the favor of the Spanish priests by working as a carpenter in the missions and by serving in the Mexican army. The only non-Mexican man so honored, Yount was the recipient of a land grant of 11,814 acres from Mariano Vallejo. (Courtesy Napa County Historical Society.)

YOUNT BLOCKHOUSE. Working with his indigenous helpers, Yount built a blockhouse and adobe dwelling in 1837. He planted wheat and orchards and raised cattle and sheep. Yount built and operated the first flour mill in 1837, called Star of the Pacific, which produced up to 30 barrels of flour per day. He planted his first vineyard using stock from a mission grapevine brought over by Spaniards and Mexicans. (Courtesy Napa County Historical Society.)

JESSE BARNETT. Jesse Barnett was the son of Elias Barnett, who came to Pope Valley and brought the first fruit tree seedling from Missouri to Calistoga in 1848, later marrying the first female settler of Pope Valley, Juliana Salazar Pope Barnett. The Barnetts, along with other Pope Valley settlers, raised cattle, horses, sheep and hogs. (Courtesy Napa County Historical Society.)

HENRIETTA CLARK HARRIS (1860–1944) AND JOE HARRIS (1858–1933). Henrietta was the daughter of Abraham Clark, who arrived in Napa in 1864 from England. By 1870, Clark was the farmer with the most land in the county—10,000 acres on which he raised wheat, cattle, hogs, and sheep. He gave his daughter Henrietta 1,000 acres of land with the condition that it could not be sold during her lifetime. Harris Canyon on the east side of Lake Berryessa is the land Clark gave his daughter. (Courtesy Judy Ann Ahmann.)

HARRIS RANCH IN BERRYESSA. The men in Henrietta's family are pictured here. From left to right are Glenn Clark, Joseph Moore, Howard Clark earmarking calf, Herbert Church, Curtis Clark, and "Prunes" Clark on horse. Though cattle and wheat were the major products, pear orchards and vineyards were planted in the 1920s. (Courtesy Judy Ann Ahmann.)

EARLY NAPA PASTURE. This is the 1866 view of Napa City from the courthouse looking west. Within the town itself, according to Henry Wigger, "Everybody had their own milk cows, chickens, and vegetable gardens. Frank Noyes had a cow up there where the Bank of America on First Street is now." (Courtesy Napa County Historical Society.)

BUTCHER SHOP AND SALOON. Saloons and butcher shops were important early businesses because of the continuity of cattle ranching from the Californio into the American settler period. Pictured is the Fagenbeyer Saloon with gunsmith Bob West and owner Oscar Fagenbeyer, and Evens Meat Shop with butchers Will O'Connell and Ed Kathan and bookkeeper Mark Pearch. In 1872, Napa had four fruit and nut stores, five hardware and agricultural implement stores, three butchers, two wine depots, two wine cellars, four plow and wagon manufactures, two feed stables, four grain warehouses, one steam mill, one brewery, and 27 bars. (Courtesy Napa County Historical Society.)

Joseph S. Hatton
1902-03

Charles H. Tinsley
1907-09

JOSEPH (J.S.) HATTON AND C.H. TINSLEY. On September 30, 1865, Rev. John Jamison Moore, founding pastor of the first AME Zion Church in California, visited members of the African American community in Napa Valley, including community leader Edward Hatton, Joseph's father. Moore's observations were printed in the *Elevator*: "Our greatest pleasure was to find in the Valley, within a radius of 10 miles from Napa, so many industrious colored farmers." Among these were Isabel Holman, who cultivated 100 acres with nine head of stock and raised 1,500 sacks of wheat; and Jacob Sinclair, who had 200 acres with 40 head of stock and 2,500 sacks of wheat and barley. (Courtesy C. Prince Hall F&AM, Firmer Lodge No. 27, Vallejo.)

DELILAH BEASLEY. This pioneer historian, who wrote *The Negro Trail Blazers of California*, included Edward Hatton's son Joseph and his wife, Esther, among her list of pioneers. In 1885, the *Napa Register* noted that Joseph, "the pioneer tonsorial artist of Napa," had "left the tools of his trade for those of the rancher and may be seen these days in the hills above Dry Creek clearing land, building fences and doing other things preliminary to settling down and enjoying farm life." (Courtesy *John Grider's Century* by Sharon McGriff-Payne.)

CHINESE FAMILY. In the late 1800s, Chinese laborers came by the hundreds to the Napa Valley to pick blackberries every July. Even more came for the hop harvest in August. By fall, these workers were no longer just field hands, but had advanced into winemaking. According to the 1883 *St. Helena Star*, by fall at least 40 were working as semipermanent "cellar rats" at the Charles Krug winery, where they earned the standard dollar without board. (Courtesy Napa County Historical Society.)

JOSS HOUSE ALTAR. The two-story Joss House, or Taoist Temple, was both a spiritual and social center for the Chinese in Napa. Its altar arrived in Napa on a sailing ship along with a wooden scroll reading, "Your blessings are spread out to embrace us all." The 200 Chinese men who worked at the Sawyer Tannery, along with those who built stone walls along Silverado Trail, created hand-carved pieces to decorate the altar. Shuck Chan donated the altar to the Chinese Historical Society in San Francisco. (Courtesy Napa County Historical Society.)

CHINESE CAMP. Napa's "Chinatown" was on a low-lying strip of land between the Napa River and Napa Creek which frequently flooded. The Chinese constructed buildings from old shingles, broken packing boxes, and flattened kerosene cans. They established a steam laundry, a barber shop, and a grocery store. Up to 300 Chinese lived there in the 1880s. Their red-uniformed band performed at funerals and New Year's festivals. More than 100 Chinese immigrants are buried at Tulocay Cemetery. (Courtesy Napa County Historical Society.)

AERIAL VIEW OF ASYLUM. The Napa Asylum (now known as the Napa State Hospital) was founded in 1876 as a model for the nation in the treatment of madness. Although many communities vied to be chosen as the site of the new asylum, Napa was selected for its climate, access to the river, and cheap land. The area purchased included a wharf on the river, a siding at the railroad tracks, and a duck ranch. (Courtesy Napa County Historical Society.)

ASYLUM WITH ORCHARDS. The patients worked in the pear orchards that ran all the way down to the river on the hundreds of acres surrounding the hospital. The beef operation outside Yountville provided meat for the Veterans' Home and the prison at San Quentin. The asylum also included a ranch and poultry farm on Coombsville Road. (Courtesy Napa County Historical Society.)

WHEAT THRESHING AMERICAN CANYON, GEORGE ROUND'S RANCH. Smith Brown bought land from Cayetano Juarez in 1858, on which to grow wheat. While once indigenous people had harvested wheat at the missions using wild horses, now it could be done with machinery pulled by domestic horses. (Courtesy Vallejo Naval and Historical Museum.)

BALE MILL. Edward Bale, an English physician, married Dona Maria Ignacia Soberanes, niece of Gen. Mariano Vallejo, and became a Mexican citizen in March 1841. He then petitioned Vallejo for a land grant, which extended from south of St. Helena to the foothills of Calistoga. This fertile acreage, called Calajomanas by the Indians, was renamed Rancho Carne Humana. The mill he built in 1847 is the only surviving one of its kind in the county. Initially built to grind grain into flour, the mill came to be a place where people could gather to visit, exchange gossip, and hold social events. (Courtesy Napa County Historical Society.)

STODDARD MILLING. In 1873, C.A. Menefee commented, "There are fewer localities in the world where wheat will grow better than in the Napa Valley . . . nearly the whole of the land in the valley is adapted to all kinds of cereals." William Stoddard traveled west by wagon train from Michigan and settled in Napa in 1880. With his sons, he soon established a prosperous grain and feed business which became one of the largest in the region, milling barley and corn. Farmers piled the grain onto horse-drawn wagons and drove it to mills like Stoddard's. (Courtesy Napa County Historical Society.)

LOVINA CYRUS. In 1846, the Cyrus family traveled overland to California with a group that included the Nash family. Lovina's daughter Mary Cyrus married William Nash. Along with Florentine Erwin Kellogg, the Nashes planted the valley's first orchards in 1840. They built a shanty of slabs from the Bale Kilburn sawmill and lived there while building their next home, called Walnut Grove. While Mary raised 12 children, William experimented with grafting, bee keeping, and the use of deep cultivation to replace irrigation. In 1848, the Nashes sold 100 peaches for $100; by 1853, their imported English walnuts became a valued crop. In 1868, they bought Magnolia Farm near Napa which they developed as a model farm. (Courtesy *Calistoga* by John Waters Jr. and Sharpsteen Museum.)

JOHN CYRUS, FATHER OF MARY CYRUS NASH. Along the road later known as the St. Helena Highway are some of the first fruit trees planted in the valley: walnut, peach, pear, orange, and olive. The remaining walnut and olive trees are more than 100 years old. (Courtesy *Calistoga* by John Waters Jr. and Sharpsteen Museum.)

PRODUCE WAGON. In the 1850s, produce was hauled by mule teams from the valley into the City of Napa. Travelers had to swim their horses across the Napa River until ferries began to operate in 1848 at Third Street. In 1850, the first steamship, *The Dolphin*, began to run from

Napa to San Francisco, carrying hay, lumber, coal, and passengers. (Courtesy Napa County Historical Society.)

CHARLES AYER HOUSE. Ayers opened the first dairy in Calistoga and built this two-story house in 1875 on Lincoln and Myrtle Streets. William Gibbs bought the property where he built a processing plant for prunes, so they did not have to be dried by individual farmers on prune trays. Gibbs leased ground on Lake Street near Railroad Avenue and moved his drying plant there; the area was known later as Pruneville. (Courtesy Woran Deckard.)

FIELD AND PLOW. Joseph Amato writes, "Farmyards were stages for concerts of sound. Doors squeaked and slammed. Boards were sawed and hammered. Boots made great sucking sounds when pulled out of the mud. Sweeping was a snare drum, raising clouds of dust. Rocks were broken and foundations were poured. Restive horses whinnied and neighed, cows bellowed . . . all the while the clinking and sucking pump filled buckets with splashing and swirling water." (Courtesy Napa County Historical Society.)

View of the R.B. Woodward Estate at Oak Knoll, 1870. Oak Knoll farm originally formed part of the Rancho de Napa land grant; it took first prize in 1856 competition for Best Farm in California under Tyther. R.B. Woodward bought the farm in 1862, keeping Tyther as his farm manager to oversee what had been, at that time, one of the largest orchards in California. (Courtesy Napa County Historical Society.)

Pear Tree, Oak Knoll. Under farm manager Richard Tyther, Oak Knoll was turned into a private agricultural experiment inspired by Luther Burbank's experiments with garden crops in Santa Rosa. (Courtesy Napa County Historical Society)

SOUTHERN PACIFIC RAILROAD TRAIN, OAKVILLE, LATE 1880S. With the development of high-speed freight service to the east coast in 1869, Napa's fruit production expanded, creating a major agricultural industry. The glamour that out-of-state consumers attached to fruit from California added to the boost in sales. (Courtesy *Yountville* by Pat Alexander and the Napa Valley Museum.)

WEBBER HOUSE. The Webber farmhouse and barn were originally located on the ranch of Captain John Grigsby, who once owned much of present day Yountville. In the 1890s, the buildings were moved to their present location on the corner of Webber Avenue and Jefferson Street in Yountville. This image shows Nancy Grigsby Webber at work in her garden there. (Courtesy Barbara and Bud Dulinsky.)

ORCHARD AND PLOW SPRING. A 1906 pamphlet noted that "Mr. H Lyons raised eighty and one half tons of grapes and sold them at $30.00 a ton . . . Mr. R.J. Trader took four thousand sixty boxes of apples . . . Mr. L.L. Short took ten tons of prunes per acre at $15.00 a ton . . . Crawford took twenty-seven tons of peaches that sold for $15.00 per ton . . . Mr. Hunter secured seventy-five tons of dried prunes that sold for $60.00 a ton . . . and John Cain gathered 60 tons of prunes at $16.00 per ton." (Courtesy Napa County Historical Society.)

SUMMIT WINERY. The first records of vineyard plantings on Spring Mountain Road date back to 1869. In 1872, the US government deeded Summit Ranch to its first owners. Current owners Pride Mountain Vineyards write, "Each Sunday, families would come to picnic, tell stories, and play cards in the large shaded area adjacent to the winery . . . Only deer, fox, coyotes, rattlesnakes, bears, and mountain lions have been continual residents." (Courtesy Napa County Historical Society.)

39

JAPANESE PERSIMMONS, OAK KNOLL. Woodward hired Jose Mateus, who had emigrated from Portugal, as his wine and brandy maker. Mateus left Oak Knoll in 1877 to establish his own winery in Napa City. (Courtesy Napa County Historical Society.)

FARMING ON SILVERADO TRAIL. Farmer John Hoffman wrote, "When I came to Napa 50 years ago, French prunes were the common variety, but some farmers grew sugar prunes . . . About 100 of the 1,700 prune trees on our farm were of the sugar variety . . . We still grow a few sugar prunes and sell them fresh at our fruit stand, where knowledgeable customers snap them up. Most people assume a prune has to be dry and wrinkled. This is not the case as we Californians know. Plums that have such high sugar content that they will dry in the sun without spoiling, are known as prunes even before they are dried." (Courtesy Napa County Historical Society.)

GROEZINGER WINERY, 1870. German-born San Francisco wine merchant Gottlieb Groezinger constructed the first large-capacity wine cellar complex in Napa Valley. The estate included a distillery built with bricks made in Yountville, a stable and barn, a cream-of-tartar manufacturing center, and a steam power plant. The winery was converted to the Vintage 1870 complex in 1968. (Courtesy Napa County Historical Society.)

JOSEPH MATHEWS WINERY. In 1882, Joseph Mateus built the Lisbon Winery, which was known for its sherry. Located at 1720 Brown Street, it is the only former downtown winery still intact. Mateus constructed the building from native stone quarried east of the city. An accomplished stonemason, Mateus built the decorative arches of the doorways himself. By the end of the 19th century, he had lost the business in a gambling game in San Francisco. The structure has been converted to the Jarvis Conservatory. (Courtesy Cathy Mathews.)

Three

WALNUTS, BARLEY, AND APPLE CIDER

1881–1930

AMONG THE ORCHARDS
by Archibald Lampman

Already in the dew-wrapped vineyards dry
Dense weights of heat press down. The large bright drops
Shrink in the leaves. From dark acacia tops
The nuthatch flings his short reiterate cry;
And ever as the sun mounts hot and high
Thin voices crowd the grass. In soft long strokes
The wind goes murmuring through the mountain oaks.
Faint wefts creep out along the blue and die.
I hear far in among the motionless trees—
Shadows that sleep upon the shaven sod—
The thud of dropping apples. Reach on reach
Stretch plots of perfumed orchard, where the bees
Murmur among the full-fringed golden-rod,
Or cling half-drunken to the rotting peach.

CONN FAMILY AT CONN RANCH, CONN VALLEY, FRONT YARD, LATE SUMMER 1890. Diane Dillon's great-grandmother Emma lived on her parents' ranch in Conn Valley after she married, and Dillon's grandmother Ivy was born there. Ivy herself described this photograph: Mrs. Myers and her daughter; Mary Conn; Emma Conn holding Emma Grace Hobson; George Myron Hobson; Ivy

Leona Hobson standing in front of him; Lena Legay; Connelly Conn; four unknown individuals. The Conn Ranch was sold about 1900, and the family moved to a farm on north side of Redwood Road. (Courtesy Diane Dillon.)

FREDERICK AND MARY VOLZ. In 1881, German-born businessman Frederick Volz and his wife, Mary Magdalena, bought 188 acres a mile south of the Veteran's Home. Volz financed the purchase from interest earned from the National Brewery in San Francisco. (Courtesy Phyllis Vallerga.)

VIEW FROM VOLZ FAMILY RANCH, LOOKING SOUTHEAST, C. 1881. The Volz ranch was located between the Veteran's Home and the Grigsby property. The Volz family was able to keep the ranch until 1972. In this period farmers grew wheat, grapes, hops, barley, and corn. (Courtesy Phyllis Vallerga.)

J.J. Sweet Trade Card. Napa's abundant fruit trees provided the ingredients for the products sold in downtown stores like J.J. Sweet, advertised here. In 1870, Herman Schwartz opened his hardware store in Napa. Schwartz sold stoves, glass, and fruit cans "at San Francisco prices," as well as agricultural equipment, making his establishment a gathering place for farmers and fishermen. (Courtesy Mr. M.)

J. J. SWEET,
Dealer in FRUITS, NUTS, CONFECTIONERY
Toys and Fancy Goods.
Main Street, Opp. Napa Bank,   NAPA CITY, CAL.

Rita Harren. Rita is pictured here at age two in a pear orchard on Redwood Road. Born in 1885, on the corner of Second and Randolph, Rita Harren Bordwell grew up to challenge the conventions about what women should do and be. Before writing her history of the labor movement in Napa, she wrote a history of the fire department and organized a firefighter museum. (Courtesy Napa County Historical Society.)

PRUNES BEING DROPPED OFF IN NAPA VIA HORSE. A slump within the fruit industry in 1868 prompted California farmers to be interested in prunes. In 1870, there were 650 acres of prune orchards in California. By 1880, the industry was well established. With the devastating impact of phylloxera on grape growing, prunes became a major contributor to the Napa County economy. (Courtesy Napa County Historical Society.)

RAY AND DOLORES JUAREZ IN THEIR BARLEY FIELD, 1896. Barley was first planted here by Mexican settlers. An Ohlone Indian living at the Santa Cruz mission described the diet: "breakfast was boiled barley; at 11 am they were given cooked horse beans and peas. At sunset they each received a ration of boiled corn." (Courtesy Napa County Historical Society.)

EIGHT MULE TEAMS OWNED BY THE VINEY RANCH. These men pose in front of an eight-mule team. According to John Callison, who was born and raised in Yountville, "Mr. Ghirardi was the last man in the valley to farm with mule teams. You could hear the mules all over town when they started braying . . . He plowed, disked, harrowed, planted, and harvested with his mules. He took the hay to his farm northwest of town and stored it in his barn." (Courtesy Lee Hart.)

CHERRY PICKERS FOR EASTERN MARKET, 1900. County Agricultural Commissioner W.D. Butler wrote in 1917: "All varieties do well in this county . . . The hardiest and most prolific is probably the Black Republican. The Tartarian and kindred varieties do well but the king of them all for profit is the Bing. The Lambert is possibly a finer cherry as to size, but so far has been a shy bearer. It might do better as the tree gets older . . . As for the Royal Anne, it does not do better anywhere. The tree is thrifty and bears well and always stands in good favor with canners as to quality. A person who understands the same can also ship them for profit, usually in excess of canning prices." (Courtesy Napa County Historical Society.)

NAPA CANNING COMPANY. The Napa Interurban Railroad was built in 1905, eventually traveling all the way up the valley. The trains ran hourly, providing affordable transportation for cannery workers as well as for the rest of the townspeople. (Courtesy Napa County Historical Society.)

ARTHUR PROUTY AND ELMER BICKFORD. The two men are planting black walnut trees on Sonoma Highway as part of a community service project for the Rotary Club. Elmer Bickford arrived in 1886. He and his wife, Ada Easterby, had a son named Robert in 1904 and a daughter named Ruth in 1907. Ruth would later help found the Napa County Historical Society. In 1923, the *San Francisco Chronicle* noted, "Napa County possesses what may be the oldest black walnut trees to be found in the state. These trees are indigenous to Napa County. The English walnut grafted on the black walnut makes a tree which will bear for over a hundred years. Napa County took first prize at the Panama-Pacific Exposition with nuts produced by J.H. Wheeler. The district around St. Helena seems to be the most favored." (Courtesy Napa County Historical Society.)

HERMAN DARMS AND MISS SODERMAN, DARMS RANCH, 1910. C.H. Menefee wrote that Herman Darms "came to California in 1883 . . . where he bought a ranch of sixty-four acres five miles north of Napa on the St. Helena road. In the early days the land had been devoted to grain raising, but later a large acreage had been converted to vineyard and a specialty was made of the grape industry. When the vineyards ceased to be profitable the vines were removed and fruit trees were planted. The principal varieties to be found on the farm at this writing are prunes, peaches, pears, and cherries." (Courtesy Napa County Historical Society.)

FRUITS, VEGETABLES, ETC.

Green	Amount-lbs Total Production	Value	DRIED	Amount-lbs	Value	CANNED	Amount Cases	Value
Apples.......	2,800,000	24,000	Almonds......	100,000	11,000	APPLES.		
Apricots.....	900,000	13,500	Apples........	90,000	1,800	Apricots...		
Asparagus....	5,000	300	Apricots.....	80,000	6,400	Blackbrs.		
Blackberries..	40,000	1,600	Blackbrs.....	0	—	Beans....		
Beans........	300,000	4,000	Beans........			Corn....		
Beets........	500,000	7,500	Chestnuts....			Cherries...		
Cabbage......	80,000	800	Currants.....			Figs....		
Celery.......	9,000	135	Cherries.....	6,000	420	Goosebrs.		
Cauliflower..	9,000	135	Figs.........			Grapes..		
Corn........	5,000,000	66,667	Goosebrs.....			Nectarines.		
Currants.....			Grapes.......			Pears....		
Cherries.....	600,000	30,000	Nectarines...			Peaches...		
Figs........			Onions.......			Peas....		
Goosebrs.....			Pears........	300,000	16,500	Plums....		
Grapes.......	26,466,666	200,000	Peaches......	120,000	6,000	Raspbrs..		
Grape Fruit..			Peanuts......			Strawbrs..		
Limes(boxes)..			Peas.........			Tomatoes.	10,000	37.50
Lemons.(boxes).			Plums........	20,000	140	Tomatoes		
Loganbrs.....	4,000	160	Prunes.......	7,500,000	342,000	(Catsup)	60,000	3600
Nectarines...	2,000	25	Raspbrs......					
Onions.......	200,000	2,000	Raisins......					
Oranges(boxes).			Strawbrs.....					
Olives.......			Walnuts......					
Pears........	4,200,000	42,000						
Peaches......	3,200,000	32,000						
Peas........	10,000	300						
Persimmons...	6,000	240						
Plums........	600,000	780						
Irish Potatoes	50,000	25,000						
Prunes.......	19,000,000	40,000						
Quinces......	50,000	400						
Raspbrs......								
Strawbrs.....	40,000	2,000						
Tomatoes.....	300,000	1,500						
TOTAL........	67,341,666	722,762	TOTAL........	8,156,000	315,020	TOTAL......		7350

CROP REPORT, 1911–1912. Prunes topped the charts for most fruit grown in Napa County this year, second only to grapes. (Courtesy Napa County Historical Society.)

PICKING RAISINS. "Our climate is peculiarly adapted to the drying of fruits and raisins . . . Dr. DK Rule of St Helena and WH Crabbe of Oakville have cured raisins which are superior to any of the imported article. The grape mostly used for raisins has been Muscat of Alexandria," wrote C.H. Menefee in 1874. (Courtesy Mr. M.)

JUDGE JOHN DEHAVEN AND FAMILY, 1912. In 1896, Mr. DeHaven purchased 25 acres of land originally owned by Salvador Vallejo. The estate included the four-room house pictured here. From left to right are Judge DeHaven, Zeruah DeHaven, daughter Sarah, granddaughter Lee DeHaven Atwood, and son Joe DeHaven. (Courtesy Dr. Jim Atwood.)

NORTHWEST VIEW OF BROWNS VALLEY, SPRING 1911. Elmer and Robert Bickford stand on Clark Hill behind Connolly Ranch overlooking prune orchards in Browns Valley. Elmer Bickford wrote to the *Register* in the 1920s, describing the bird counting expeditions he had taken with his Boy Scout troop in Napa County. Bickford and his troop counted several hundred species, many of which have now disappeared. (Courtesy Robert Northrop.)

AGRICULTURAL CLASS AT PACIFIC UNION COLLEGE, 1914. Student farmers gather at Pacific Union College on Howell Mountain, around 1914. In 1909, the Seventh Day Adventist Church purchased the Angwin Resort in the mountains above St. Helena. The church bought the land and its buildings for $60,000, and PUC was dedicated at its present Angwin site on September 29, 1909. (Courtesy Pacific Union College.)

PICKING CHERRIES. Cherries were an important part of Napa's agricultural production. W.D. Butler wrote in 1917, "The oldest trees in the county are still thrifty and bear well . . . By keeping all deadwood removed, the tree keeps sending out new wood. Trees that are over forty years old have as nice tops as ever . . . A cherry orchard is the nicest and easiest of orchards to care for. It requires little pruning and usually no spraying. Soil beneath cherry trees cultivates easily because of the shade which keeps the soil from sun baking." (Courtesy Napa Valley Historical Society.)

EXHIBIT AT THE CALIFORNIA CHERRY CARNIVAL IN SANTA CLARA, JUNE 2–6, 1914. Napa Chamber of Commerce took first prize for its cherries at the California Cherry Carnival in Santa Clara. The valleys of Napa Creek and Redwood Creek were especially heavily planted with the Chapman cherry, developed by a man of that name in Browns Valley. (Courtesy Napa County Historical Society.)

California Fruit Growers Convention
Napa Cal- Nov- 15.16.17.1916.
Chasteen Photographer.

CALIFORNIA FRUIT GROWERS CONVENTION, NAPA, NOVEMBER 15–17, 1916. In 1923, the *San Francisco Chronicle* noted, "The Bartlett pear crop of Napa County is marketed about equally in three ways. One-third is shipped fresh to Eastern Markets . . . Another third of the crop goes direct to the canneries . . . the remaining third of the production is dried. Bartlett pears begin to produce for market in their fourth year, and continue to increase in production until their tenth year, when they are considered to be full bearing." (Courtesy Napa County Historical Society.)

MT. GEORGE FARM CENTER FRUIT DISPLAY. In 1867, Oliver Hudson Kelley organized the Order of Patrons of Husbandry. Membership was open to both men and women, and each local group was known as a Grange. The goal was to present news of educational value to farmers at their meetings. In 1923, the *San Francisco Chronicle* reported, "These farm centers are also mediums for social interchange, 'getting acquainted' in a way that is pleasant and often produces life-long friendships . . . Newly arrived settlers will be interested in Mount George Farm Center in particular, because it is the 'daddy' of them all, having been the very first established in the United States." These one-story buildings had kitchens donated by farming families. (Courtesy Napa County Historical Society.)

56

MT. GEORGE FARM CENTER. Herman Baade, an agriculture teacher at Napa High School, began giving lectures at the Grange in 1914 as a member of the UC Agricultural Extension Service in an effort to take the teachings and results of research work in agriculture nearer to rural people. Baade helped to organize over a dozen centers where farmers met to share ideas. Napa County farm centers were in the following areas: Browns Valley, Los Carneros, Las Amigas, Coombsville, Salvador, Soscol, Oak Knoll, along with Rutherford Grange in Rutherford, and the Tucker Farm Center in Calistoga. (Courtesy Napa County Historical Society.)

GEORGE L. THRONE PEAR SPRAYING CREW, C. 1911. George's parents bought their property in the late 1880s while living in Arizona. His father, William, died before they could move, but by 1900 George's widowed mother, Lanora, was living on the land with her five children. She died in 1904 when George was only 19; he ultimately took over the farm. The Throne family farm was in and around (to the north) of the "century oak" in Browns Valley (almost across the street from Browns Valley Market). (Courtesy Diane Dillon.)

GEORGE L. THRONE PRUNE DIPPING, C. 1911. In 1910, George married Ivy Hobson, the daughter of George Myron Hobson and Emma (Conn) Hobson, who had a farm on the north side of Redwood Road, near the T intersection with Browns Valley Road. Diane Dillon says, "I have my grandfather George's dance card from a dance at the Browns Valley Farm Center from before my grandparents married . . . and Ivy is his first and last dance." (Courtesy Diane Dillon.)

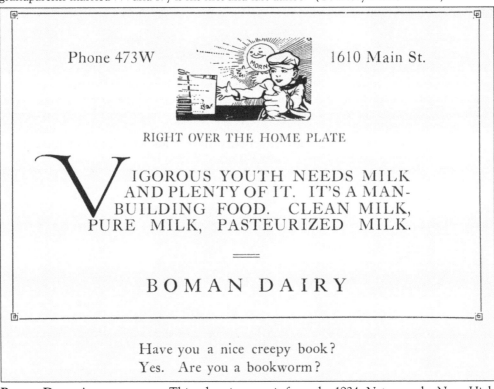

BOMAN DAIRY ADVERTISEMENT. This advertisement is from the 1924 *Napanee*, the Napa High School yearbook. Dairy wagons traveled daily through Napa, Sonoma, and Solano Counties. The *San Francisco Chronicle* reported in 1923 that there were 19,000 dairy cows in the county: "There is good pasture condition. The southwestern part of the county is principally a dairy country. Plenty of alfalfa can be grown as well as hay. There is a creamery at Napa and one at Calistoga and there are good facilities for shipping milk and cream." (Courtesy Robert Northrup.)

RECEIPT FOR SALE OF EGGS, 1928. Eggs from the Luhmann farm were shipped to San Francisco. Henry and his wife, Beatrice, pitched their tent downtown when they first came to town by covered wagon in 1913 and then bought their land at 2275 Big Ranch Road. Beatrice wrote, "Planted a young orchard of prune trees, while we were waiting for fruit went into the chicken business. The babies survived—that meant more chickens. My upbringing was never buy anything you don't need, if you owe money. We had a mortgage and with crop failures and low prices for poultry to make ends meet, we raised fryers, the whole sale price was so low we dressed them, price 20 cents a pound for the pan and delivered, that was my job, at the crack of dawn would dress from 100 to 300 in the morning and deliver in the afternoon." (Courtesy Deb Jachens.)

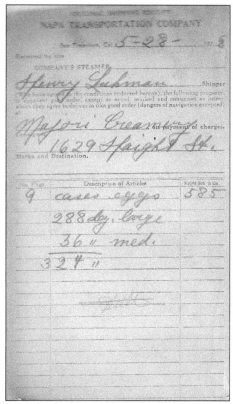

CHICKEN FARM IN CALISTOGA. In 1923, the *San Francisco Chronicle* noted that Napa's main poultry district lay east of the Napa River, adjacent to the mountains. "It extends almost the entire length of the valley," estimating 100,000 poultry in Napa County. (Courtesy Napa County Historical Society.)

SUSCOL RANCH APPLE ORCHARD. These trees were near the site of Thompson's Gardens, whose 150,000 trees were famous all over California. (Courtesy Napa County Historical Society.)

BLAUFUSS APPLE CIDER WORKS. Here apples were processed into cider, and on Little Trancas Road, another plant processed cherries into maraschino cherries, put them in barrels and shipped them by rail to bottling plants. George Blaufuss's business was located at what is now Embassy Suites. (Courtesy Napa County Historical Society.)

DELANEY PRUNE RANCH, ST. HELENA. Lelia
Ashleigh Delaney (left) and sister Laura Amelia
Delaney in front of the Delaney Ranch, on a
rare Napa snow day in late 1934. In 1915 and
1918, Amelia Lipp Delaney bought 34 acres
along Stice Lane in South St. Helena. She was
married to a Mare Island worker and was a
mother of four when she began planting prunes.
Amelia marketed the fruit through California
Prune and Apricot Growers, a cooperative
founded in 1917. The co-op sold dried fruit,
and by 1932, prune juice to Sunsweet. When
she died in 1940, the trees she had planted
yielded 5,700 pounds of prunes. (Courtesy Marie
Meyer Bowen.)

NAPA STATE HOSPITAL, 1930s. The Asylum, renamed Napa State Hospital in 1922, operated
prosperous orchards for decades. Although Napa Junior College's founding president Harry
McPherson was instrumental in obtaining approval of a bond to purchase 150 acres of the land,
he also mourned the loss of the farm where asylum residents harvested the fruit. (Courtesy
Cathy Mathews.)

BROWNS VALLEY PRUNE TREES. By 1928, the Napa Valley prune crop was worth twice as much as its wine grapes. Brown's Valley looked like this until the middle of the 20th century. (Courtesy Napa County Historical Society.)

GEORGE L. THRONE'S PRUNE DRYING YARD, 1926. Throne's granddaughter Diane Dillon writes, "The little girl in the photo is my mother (born in 1922, age four at time of photo) Georgina Ivy Throne; her father (George L. Throne) and dog are on left side of photo. My mother married John Dillon in 1943 in Napa." George and Ivy met at a dance at the Dream Bowl. They lost the farm to foreclosure during the Great Depression. Diane remembers journeying to visit the old property: "My mother would drive me when I was a child, or in her later years, have me drive her, out First Street, to Browns Valley Road, to pause and look at the Century Oak, and talk about the family farm." (Courtesy Diane Dillon.)

Four

Pear and Prune Growers All

1931–1960

Fresh Prune Torte

Recipe from Jobyna Carpenter (sister-in-law of Dorothy Wurz)
submitted by Dorothy Wurz from Wurz Ranch

Cream 1 cup sugar with ½ cup butter plus 2 eggs.
Sift together: 1 cup flour, 1 tsp baking powder, pinch of salt.
Add above together a little at a time.
Fold in nuts (optional).
Spray 8x8-inch baking pan with Pam.
It will be a thick batter.
Use 24 halves of fresh prunes, pushing them down into batter
    skin side up.
Sprinkle with cinnamon and lemon juice.
Bake 1 hour in a 350-degree oven.

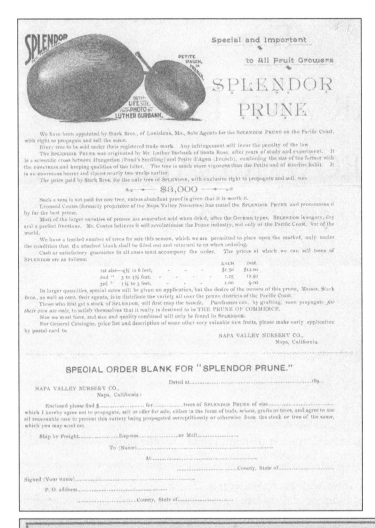

PRUNE ORDER FORM. A group of Napa growers organized the Napa Mutual Dehydrator in 1932, which operated until 1950. Ninety percent of Napa prune, pear, and cherry growers belonged to an association. (Courtesy Napa County Historical Society.)

DIRT FARMER ADVERTISEMENT, 1939. In the March 3, 1939, edition of *Dirt Farmer*, a newspaper devoted to the agricultural industry in Napa County, farming and agricultural supply stores advertised their businesses. (Courtesy Napa County Historical Society.)

LOUIS WURZ AND MACK CLEMMONS, WURZ PRUNE RANCH, OLD SONOMA HIGHWAY. In 1941, Dorothy Wurz worked at Walch's Creamery on Main Street in Napa. She recalls a very handsome young man, Al Wurz, who would come in with his best friend, Joe Hill. The men worked for Lou Wurz Sr. who started planting prune trees in the 1930s. The two became lifelong friends and partners in farming operations around the valley. Al and Dorothy started going together in 1942 and married soon after. Like many farmers back then, her father-in-law planted apple, cherry, and pear trees to supplement the family's income. "We had four kids and we all worked picking prunes. It was kind of a dirty job—and hot." (Courtesy Dorothy Wurz.)

OLAMAE WADE AND FAMILY. When Olamae was three years old, a flood washed her family's house down a river, so they left Texas and came to Napa in 1924. The family pitched a tent at Gardner's Auto Camp along Napa Creek. In 1928, they rented a farm house in Browns Valley where prune orchards stretched "as far as you could see," and where she and her brothers picked prunes. She attended Browns Valley School, a one-room school with eight grades and 26 students, who were kept warm by a wood-burning stove. (Courtesy Olamae Wade Combelleck.)

OLAMAE WADE AND FAMILY PICNICKING AT THE END OF PARTRICK ROAD, SURROUNDED BY APRICOT TREES. In 1921, *The Napa Register* noted, "The finest apricots grown in the State are those now being harvested at Morton Duhig's ranch in Carneros district . . . This most significant statement was made in the presence of Mr. Duhig and farm advisor H.J. Baade, who witnessed the tests on the apricots. The cots were declared to be unequalled for flavor and other qualities anywhere. Apricots at the Duhig ranch and other orchards in Las Amigas have won the admiration of local fruit experts in the past, but it was not until Professor Horne completed his surveys yesterday that it was shown that Napa orchards raise the finest fruit of this variety in the State." (Courtesy Olamae Combelleck.)

PRUNE CREW. Olamae Wade's mother, Martine, is pictured with her prune harvest crew and employer, Mr. McKenzie. Martine was a harvest captain for the prune farms in Browns Valley. Olamae worked at the cannery pitting maraschino cherries and helped her mother in the orchards. After she married Archie Combelleck, they bought land on Estee Avenue, paying for it by picking and drying 14 acres of prunes for $150 an acre. (Courtesy Olamae Combelleck.)

NAPA CHERRY SHED AT THE CORNER OF VALLEJO STREET AND LITTLE TRANCAS ROAD, 1949. Pictured are Harmon Perry, Mildred Perry, and Pat Ruff in the sorting and processing room. Frances Proctor remembers, "It was summer of 1947, and I was amazed at the orchards lining the highway coming into town. I had no idea what was on the trees, but soon found out that we would be making our living from them." (Courtesy Frances Proctor.)

BAUMAN FAMILY, YOUNTVILLE, 1930S. Rudy Bauman and daughter Lois are shown in front of their family house on Madison Street. Lois Bauman Bishop and sister Phyllis Bauman Vallerga are descendants of the pioneer Volz family. (Courtesy Phyllis Vallerga.)

WALTER KNOTT IN BOYSENBERRY FIELD. Rudolph Boysen was a farmer and amateur horticulturalist. In 1924, while living on Third Avenue, he developed the boysenberry by combining pollen from a blackberry and a loganberry or red raspberry. When he left for Anaheim in 1925, he took six vines with him, which he planted in an orange grove. His new berry was 50 percent bigger and juicier than the blackberry, but no one was interested. In 1932, scientist George Darrow went to Anaheim with berry grower Walter Knott. There they found Boysen, who led them to his vines. They transplanted them to Knott's farm, and began selling the berries at their farm stand in 1935. Knott dubbed them "boysenberries." (Courtesy Knotts Berry Farm.)

TONNAGE AND VALUES OF THE FRUIT CROP OF NAPA COUNTY FOR 1930			
KIND	TONS	VALUE	TOTAL
Apples			
Shipping	450	$ 7,000	$ 32,700
Local	400	12,000	
Dried	70	11,200	
By-products	320	2,500	
Apricots			
Green	150	$ 6,000	$ 11,000
Dry	25	5,000	
Cherries			
Shipping	225	$ 31,500	$ 130,250
Canning	525	78,750	
Local	200	20,000	
Grapes			
Interstate - 1027 cars	13,500		$ 342,000
Intrastate - 213 "	3,000		
By truck	2,500		
Pears			
Shipping - Napa	1,750	$ 26,250	$ 125,750
" - Calistoga	300	4,500	
" - Berryessa	1,750	35,000	
	3,800	65,750	
Canning	865	$ 24,250	
Dried	327	35,750	
Prunes	15,250		$ 1,067,500
Plums	100		2,000
Peaches			
Green	75	$ 2,250	7,750
Dry	50	5,500	
Tomatoes	1,800		27,000
Walnuts	100		40,000
		TOTAL VALUE	$ 1,785,950

NOTE: Compiled by
W. D. BUTLER, Agricultural Commissioner
Napa County

NAPA COUNTY CROP REPORT, 1930. The abundance of produce helped Napans avoid many of the worst aspects of the Great Depression. (Courtesy Napa County Historical Society.)

JIM GHIRARDI PREPARING TO HAUL GRAPES. According to John Callison, "He also pruned and burned Bardessono's vineyard next to the school. He used a burn wagon after pruning the vines. It was quite a sight to see the wagon with flames shooting out and smoke billowing up moving around the vineyard. It never seemed to bother his mules, however." (Courtesy Lee Hart.)

GATHERING OF LYERLAS AND FRIENDS ON MT. VEEDER, 1935. The Lyerla family operated the Lyerla Brothers Apple and Berry Farm beginning in 1928. Included in this group are Fred Lyerla on guitar, Bill Lyerla on fiddle, and Grandpa Lyerla in front center. The property is now known as Scully Ranch. (Courtesy Eugene Lyerla.)

LYERLA
BROS. APPLE
ADVERTISEMENT.
The brothers
sold their berries
in San Francisco
and their apples
at local markets,
including
their own on
the corner of
Lincoln and
Jefferson in
Napa. (Courtesy
Eugene Lyerla.)

THE LYERLA BROTHERS ON MT. VEEDER, 1945. The Lyerla Ranch had a long packing shed where apples were sorted by size, then polished and wrapped in purple tissue. (Courtesy Eugene Lyerla.)

AL WURZ AND FARM WORKER ON PRUNE ORCHARD, 1940S. Dorothy and Al Wurz lived with Louis Wurz Sr. on the family's ranch (the current location of Harvest Middle School). Al later had a prune farm where Newell's Mobile Home Park now sits on Solano Avenue. Dorothy Wurz remembers, "We had some bad years. We would think we had a really good crop, then there would be a frost, and it would be ruined. We didn't get rich, but we made a good living." (Courtesy Dorothy Wurz.)

PRUNE BOXES ON DARMS RANCH. Frank Randall came up with the idea of a dehydrator that could handle 2,500 tons of fruit. John Cantoni designed the new plant with a heating chamber, a fan, and an automatic scale. (Courtesy Napa County Historical Society.)

BARTLETT PEARS. California also contributed to peach, pear and cherry production, providing two-fifths of the nation's supply of peaches and a third of its pears. Pear production in the Pacific Coast states rose threefold between 1919 and 1938. Clingstone peaches in California represented 20–30 percent of the country's total peach crop. (Courtesy Napa County Historical Society.)

WURZ WORKERS UNLOADING PRUNES, 1940. Dorothy Wurz still resides at the end of Wurz Lane (also known as Oak Knoll West) on the acreage she shared with husband Al, where one original prune tree remains. (Courtesy Dorothy Wurz.)

TEODOSIO (THEODORE) GRANDE
WITH NEPHEW JOE ON THE FAMILY
PRUNE ORCHARD, SPRING 1944.
An immigrant from Mussolone, in
the Vincenza region of Italy, Grande
came to Napa Valley around 1910
and bought into a prune orchard and
vineyard at the corner of Lokoya and
Mt. Veeder Roads, owned by a Mr.
Menneguzzo, who had come from
his same village in Italy. (Courtesy
Dorothy Rossi.)

BLOSSOMING PEAR ORCHARD ON THE GRANDE/ROSSI RANCH, MAY 1946. After returning from
the military in 1919, Theodore Grande sold his interest in the Mt. Veeder property to purchase
land on Silverado Trail with his brother Nazareno. They bought 25 acres total, 17 acres in prunes
and three acres in pears, and five acres of grapes. (Courtesy Dorothy Rossi.)

DRYING TRAYS ON GRANDE/ROSSI FARM ON SILVERADO TRAIL. By 1942, California produced 90 percent of grapes and apricots and combined with Oregon, over 90 percent of all plums and prunes. (Courtesy Dorothy Rossi.)

INSTALLING IRRIGATION, 1942. Pacific Union College Services crew is installing irrigation system through the apple orchard. The former resort's hotel, bowling alleys, and cottages became dormitories, classrooms, and faculty homes. (Courtesy Pacific Union College.)

TRACTOR STUCK IN MUD AT PACIFIC UNION COLLEGE. Students and faculty worked together, often using lumber harvested from the college property. The campus included a dairy, a chicken farm, and offered such courses as blacksmithing and home economics. (Courtesy Pacific Union College.)

ERNEST F. KNIEF SR. AND HIS DAUGHTERS BETHEL AND CAROLYN IN FRONT OF THEIR CHERRY ORCHARD, 1942. Ernest F. Knief Sr. was born in Napa in 1894, to Louis and Caroline (Whorman) Knief. Louis's grandfather was a farmer in Browns Valley. Caroline's grandmother farmed on Soda Canyon Road. At 17, Ernest began working at Mare Island Naval Shipyard, from which he retired in 1957, as a Leading Man in Shop No. 31. Prior to his marriage to Lillian Ransford in 1934, he purchased 20 acres of land. Mr. Knief grew three types of prunes; French prunes, a small prune; Imperial prunes, large and meaty, and Sugar prunes, which were mid-sized, on the acreage north of West Park Avenue. (Courtesy Carolyn Knief Salazar.)

HENRY LUHMANN AND HIS WIFE, BEATRICE. Henry Luhmann was the chair of the Farm Council in the 1940s, dealing with problems of finding workers for the harvest during World War II; his correspondence indicates that the going rate for both Mexican nationals and domestic pickers was 70¢ an hour in 1945. The Luhmanns grew figs, prunes, and other vegetables. Beatrice saved boxes of feathers from her chickens, separated by colors, with which she would decorate hats. Marilyn Grover describes her as "energetic, animated, and generous . . . she grew beautiful orchids . . . some of her fig drying racks are still kept by her friends, including Nathan Fay's widow." (Courtesy Deb Jachens.)

EGG BROCHURE. Henry Luhmann patented an egg incubator. Friend Marilyn Grover said, "Everytime he bought something, a tool or machinery, he bought two so that when something broke he had the parts to fix it." He worked with county farmers to establish housing during World War II for agricultural laborers, who included Mexican nationals, German prisoners of war, and patients from Napa State Hospital. Henry Luhmann also successfully advocated that veterans receive surplus housing after the war ended. Their farm had a thick plank painted with big letters spelling "Luhmann." (Courtesy Deb Jachens.)

LUIS VEGA AND FAMILY. The boom in defense jobs created a labor shortage in the agricultural industry. In 1942, to address the problem, growers persuaded the federal government to create a "guest worker—or *bracero*—program in California, bringing Mexican workers to fill the labor gap. Vega came to Napa County in the 1940s as part of that program. Many *bracero* workers stayed and established families in Napa. Pictured are Vega's wife, Josefina Vega-Cuevas, and the couple's two daughters who moved to the city of Napa in 1989. (Courtesy Oscar Vega.)

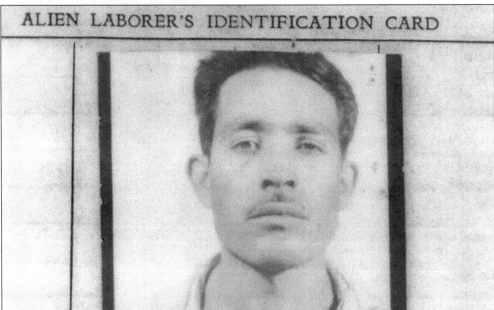

ALIEN LABORER'S IDENTIFICATION CARD

JOSE TIJERO, BRACERO. Rosa Tijero wrote, "Jose Garcia, my father, alien labor ID card, taken December 7, 1955, prior to coming to California to work in the fields of Salinas, where he toiled for 25 years, providing for his family in Mexico. In 1969, he marched with Cesar Chavez. He retired from the fields in 1985 and lives with his daughter [me] in Napa." (Courtesy Rosa Tijero.)

FRANCES PROCTOR
WITH BLACKIE ON KELLY
ROAD, 1951. "We moved
into the old German
prisoner-of-war camp on
Silverado Trail and my
mom and dad set out to
find work. They stopped
at an orchard of prune
trees just north of the old
eucalyptus trees on the
left side of Highway 29,
near Yountville. At first,
I thought this won't be
such a hard job, picking
up those little pieces of
fruit and putting them
in the box. Oh my. Was
I ever wrong." (Courtesy
Frances Proctor.)

FRANCES PROCTOR,
LATE SUMMER 1951.
"As it turns out, I
would eventually
pick prunes each
summer to buy
school clothes that I
wanted. Most of the
kids in the valley
did likewise. School
didn't start until the
fruit was in. It could
be back-breaking
work unless you
figured out a way
to ease the pain.
Mine was to sit on
my backside and
scoot around under
the trees. It was
always hot, so you
picked the shady
side first." (Courtesy
Frances Proctor.)

BATTER UP, 1953. Carolyn Knief waits for a pitch in a cornfield on the family farm. In the late 1940s, Knief's father planted corn along with a small orchard of Alberta peaches. She writes, "In the evenings, after he got home from work, and during summers, along with family and some workers, he gathered the boxes of prunes from the orchards on a flatbed truck. They brought them to the barn area to be dipped in a lye solution, and then set out to dry on trays in the sun. As the prunes dried, if they did not contain enough sugar, they would turn brown and shrivel. These brown prunes, which were called 'chocolates,' were picked from the trays and discarded. The good prunes, once dried, were sold to the Sun Sweet facilities in Napa." The family also picked and sliced the peaches, dried them in a sulfa smoke, and sold them to Sun Sweet. (Courtesy Carolyn Knief Salazar.)

CAROL RAAHAUGE, 1951. Carol (right), posed with best friends Hilde Dusen and Connie MacLean at the county fair. When she was five, her parents bought a farm in Napa, pulled out the prune trees, put in a barn, and opened the Hagen Road Dairy. Carol would milk her cows named Doris and Betty by hand. She and her family churned butter and sold milk at their drive-in store. Carol later operated the Secret Garden at the very same location at 1242 Hagen Road. (Courtesy Connie MacLean Venturi.)

DAVID WHEATLEY AND
MR. EISLEY OF SUNSWEET
GROWERS, WHEATLEY
ORCHARD, SEPTEMBER
1951. Henry Wheatley,
one of the earliest Napans
to grow prunes, emigrated
from England in 1892 and
bought 50 acres of land
just north of Napa, and
40 more acres by 1902.
When California growers
decided to develop a
state cooperative, Henry
Wheatley represented
Napa County. After
son David married in
1947, David and his
wife bought 30 acres
next to his folks and
continued to grow prunes.
Wheatley told reporter
Marcia Dorgan in 2000,
"I still prefer prunes.
They're good and healthy
for you. Before wine
grapes, the Napa Valley
supported a diversified
agriculture." (Courtesy
David Wheatley.)

CROP DUSTER. Crop Duster landing on an open field on Trancas, which stretched from where
Queen of the Valley Medical Center is now located, to the corner of Trancas and Villa Lane.
(Courtesy Cathy Mathews.)

ERNEST KNIEF'S CORNFIELD, C. 1951. Pictured from left to right are Tobin Wigington, Ernest Knief Jr., Carolyn Knief (holding the Knief dachshund, Rye), Bethel Knief, and Doug Wigington, all standing in front of Mr. Knief's cornfield. Carolyn remembers growing up, "I enjoyed spraying the prune trees to protect them from various diseases. Pop would fill the stray rig with water and the chemicals needed for the spray. We would dress up in oversized rain slickers and hats, put

some type of mask over our noses and mouths so that we would not breath in the chemicals, and climb up onto the top of the spray rig. Pop would drive his tractor, pulling the spray rig, up and down the rows of prune trees while we, holding nozzled hoses, would spray the trees." (Courtesy Carolyn Knief Salazar.)

FRANK AND FLORENCE TRATHEN ON THEIR LINDA VISTA FARM, 1959. Grace Trathen Methven's passion for 4-H and the country life began when her parents moved to the Napa Valley in 1933 after her father bought a 50-acre ranch on Linda Vista Avenue. She shared the land with her family and a host of animals, including cows, chickens, pigs, ducks, geese, rabbits, and turkeys. (Courtesy Grace Methven.)

GRACE AND HER FATHER, FRANK TRATHEN, AUGUST 1952. Here the two have just returned from the dehydrator. Prunes from their farm were hauled to Moudrie's dehydrator, which dehydrated them for 22 hours. Then a week or so later, as Grace remembers, they were "sacked" and sent to packing at Union Station on Redwood Road at Highway 29. (Courtesy Grace Methven.)

MILKING TIME, GRACE TRATHEN, 1953.
Following her introduction to farm life, Grace
joined the local branch of 4-H at age 10 and
become a volunteer leader for the organization
at age 20. The 4-H Club movement was created
by the Farm Centers in the 1920s to teach rural
children citizenship and leadership. (Courtesy
Grace Methven.)

HERMAN BAADE, COUNTY DIRECTOR OF AGRICULTURAL EXTENSION SERVICE, 1950. Grace Methven
volunteered as a camp registrar during 4-H's annual summer camping trip in Los Posadas, where
she had camped as a child. Ed Weber, director of UC Cooperative Extension, said, "I think if
you asked most 4-H members who have been to camp in the last 30 or 40 years, all of them are
going to remember Grace." In addition to 4-H, Methven volunteered as a librarian at Shearer
Elementary School, where she was a teacher for 37 years. (Courtesy Grace Methven.)

PETER GASSER. Born at home in Napa in 1905, Peter Gasser was one of six children of Swiss immigrants Henry Gasser and Mary Crotta, who had come to the United States in the late 19th century. The Gassers were farmers, and for many years his father was the head dairyman at Napa State Hospital. At their ranch in Coombsville, the family had a prune orchard, raised turkeys and chickens, and operated a dairy with goats and cows. (Courtesy Peter and Vernice Gasser Foundation.)

VERNICE (PAT) STODDARD GASSER. William Stoddard [Chapter Two] died when daughter Vernice was only 11, leaving her mother Isabelle Ilos Stoddard to successfully carry on the milling business. Daughter Vernice (Pat) married Peter Gasser and became a community leader. Early in World War II, she became involved with war relief organizations and, along with other volunteers, opened a salvage shop, so successful that it continued to operate on behalf of the Napa community and became Community Projects Inc. (Courtesy Peter and Vernice Gasser Foundation.)

GASSER'S MIRACLE MILE: SOSCOL AVENUE, LATE 1940S. In 1954, Pete Gasser's auto dealership relocated from Second and Randolph to this former farm land. In 1975, there was a fruit stand on the corner of Soscol and Highway 29, and all the rest was open fields. (Courtesy Napa County Historical Society).

CATTLE. Huge cattle ranches sprawled over Napa County's borders into Solano County. Cattlemen worked in cooperation with one another. Rancher Roy Mason remembers, "We would order our cattle from Utah, and shipments would come in on the railroad at the station where Scandia is now. Whenever any of the big ranches had a herd coming in, all the other ranchers would meet them at the station, on horseback, and we'd help them drive the cattle to their ranches in Monticello or Napa." (Courtesy Napa County Historical Society.)

DEBORAH AND HOWARD JACHENS AND CALF, 1960. Brother and sister are pictured on Justice Benkiser's land, originally 1,200 acres at the end of Redwood Road. Jachens comments, "They always had cattle on the land. You ran cattle for food, would let them graze, then round them up and bring them in for branding. After they were killed they were taken to Giovannoni's on Brown Street to be hung." (Courtesy Deb Jachens.)

HAROLD JACHENS. Howard and Deborah's grandfather patrolled the land by jeep to check fence lines and water troughs. (Courtesy Deb Jachens.)

88

Five

Saving Rural History

1961–1989

ODE TO CONNOLLY RANCH
by Peggy Wilson Aaron

Was it the first trip into California as fruit tramps
from Oklahoma, Missouri, Arkansas
that early memory became collective memory
of Apples in Washington, Peaches in Yuba, Cherries in Stockton
Prunes in Napa?

Children in back seats sleep in the early light
while parents keep to the task
reaping the harvests for the landed
so safe, so secure.

Years of labor and desire for a better life
We have come so far, morphing again to find connection to the land
reaping again the harvest (but always for the landed)
Apples in Washington, Peaches in Yuba, Prunes in Napa
or is it Grapes?
The memory grows dim.

Seventy years later in the Napa Valley it is time for the farmer's market
Second Tuesday or Third Thursday
we have forgotten how to grow, how to pick, how to preserve
but not to worry, it is time for the farmer's market
Third Tuesday, or Second Thursday
Heirloom tomatoes, fresh herbs, succulent fruit
And we remember that we must not forget
That on Saturday we can visit Connolly Ranch.

HELEN CONNOLLY. Although they lived in San Francisco, Helen and Peggy visited their family ranch on Browns Valley Road regularly as children and young adults. Family friend Lorie Saxon remembers, "Peggy and Helen were very special and unusual people, you knew that if you knew them for more than five minutes. I remember them as being unusually intelligent women, something I was always looking for. Always a step or two ahead." (Courtesy Connolly Ranch.)

PEGGY CONNOLLY. Friend Roger Andrews (Lorie's brother) says, "Peggy and Helen were in some ways larger than life figures. They were smart—maybe brilliant. They were plain-spoken, no-nonsense women who could—and did—take on anyone who crossed them. With their brother and father, and those who worked for them occasionally at the ranch, I recall them as caring and compassionate." (Courtesy Connolly Ranch.)

RUTH VON UHLIT. Ruth Raeder moved to Napa in 1923, where her uncle was an orchardist for Napa State Hospital. Ruth worked on a ranch in the summer for a disabled World War I veteran, where she pitched hay and picked fruit. She bought her first motorcycle in 1929, for $10 and commuted to University of California at Berkeley, doing housework to pay her tuition of $25 a semester. (Courtesy Greta von Uhlit.)

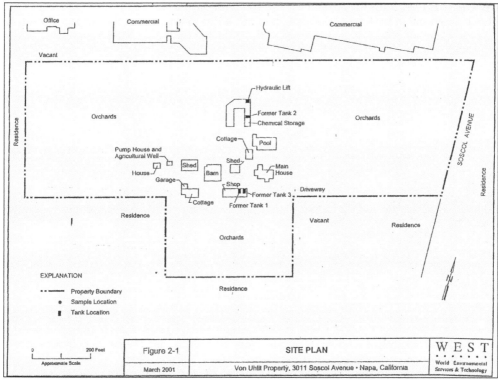

MAP OF VON UHLIT PROPERTY. Vicky Mena's family worked for Ruth von Uhlit, one of the last family farmers within the city of Napa. Active in Farming Trails, Napa County Farm Bureau, and the Napa County Agricultural Preserve Association, von Uhlit also taught citizenship classes for 33 years and attended all citizenship swearing-in ceremonies. (Courtesy Vicky Mena.)

VON UHLIT PLUMS. Ruth Raeder and George von Uhlit met at the Vichy Springs Pool in 1931. They married and in 1933, for $2,000 cash, bought a 40-acre farm on Soscol Avenue just south of Trancas, where she gave swimming lessons to the children of countless Napa families. (Courtesy Lauren Coodley.)

PANORAMIC VIEW OF THE KNIEF FARM, C. 1960. Ernest Knief Jr. took this photograph from the windmill. As Napa began to grow, it became more difficult to take the farm equipment across West Park Avenue for plowing under the prune trees, and Mr. Knief sold the 10 acres to the north of West Park Avenue in the late 1940s or early 1950s. He continued farming the other 10 acres until about 1965, when the majority of the land was sold. His daughter Carolyn remembers, "I loved riding on the flatbed truck and helping gather the boxes of prunes. I remember the nights when we would have a summer rain storm, and all the family would rush out to the fields to stack the trays of prunes so that they wouldn't get wet." (Courtesy Carolyn Knief Salazar.)

ERNEST SR. AND LILLIAN KNIEF, 1963. Carolyn Salazar remembered, "After Pop planted the wheat fields, and the grain was harvested, one year the shaft was put into bales. We had fun making forts out of the bales until they were sold. I always enjoyed riding on his caterpillar tractor with him, or riding on the drag (which leveled off the plowed ground) when he plowed our fields . . . I have fond memories of picking berries with Mom, Beth, and Ernie Jr., and all of us slicing peaches, arranging them on trays to be dried in a covering Pop had prepared. I also enjoyed helping shuck the field corn after it had dried." (Courtesy Carolyn Knief Salazar.)

SUNSWEET BOARD OF DIRECTORS, 1967. Pictured are Charlie O'Connor, Ken Clark, unidentified, Mr. Schmidt, Louis Wurz, Sr., Cecil Herrick, Hubert Frehauf, unidentified, Joe Hill, unidentified, and George Jepson. (Courtesy Joseph Hill.)

FRUIT and NUT CROPS
Production - Value

Crops		Year	Bearing Acreage	Per Acre		Total	Unit	Per Unit	Total	
APPLES	Fresh	1963				272	Tons	$170.00	$	46,240
		1962				238	Tons	120.00		28,560
	Processed	1963				231	Tons	45.00		10,395
		1962				820	Tons	30.00		24,600
	Total	1963	173	2.91	Tons	503	Tons			56,635
		1962	168	6.30	Tons	1,058	Tons			53,160
GRAPES		1963	10,025	3.23	Tons	32,382	Tons		***	3,076,290
		1962	9,800	4.03	Tons	39,516	Tons		***	3,951,600
PEARS	Canning	1963				1,232	Tons	112.00		137,984
		1962				2,025	Tons	75.00		151,875
	Processed	1963				44	Tons	60.00		2,640
		1962				804	Tons	46.50		37,386
	Total	1963	616	2.07	Tons	1,276	Tons			140,624
		1962	597	4.57	Tons	2,829	Tons			189,261
PRUNES		1963	6,355	.68	Tons	4,325	Tons	280.00		1,211,000
		1962	6,282	1.19	Tons	7,510	Tons	220.00		1,652,200
WALNUTS	English	1963				540	Tons	500.00		270,000
		1962				700	Tons	460.00		322,000
	Black	1963				50	Tons	200.00		10,000
		1962				50	Tons	100.00		5,000
	Total	1963	1,966	.30	Tons	590	Tons			280,000
		1962	1,935	.39	Tons	750	Tons			327,000
MISC. FRUITS (Berries, Peaches, Olives, Cherries, Apricots, Plums, etc.)		1963								65,000
		1962								60,000
TOTAL FRUIT AND NUT CROPS		1963								$4,829,549
		1962								$6,233,221

***Varietal prices considered in arriving at total grape income.

CROP REPORT 1962–1963. In contrast to these figures, by the 1990s grapes were 99 percent of production. (Courtesy Napa County Historical Society.)

JOE HILL, 1962. Joe was a Kansas wheat farmer who came to Napa in 1941 at the age of 19. He made a prewar deposit on 48 acres on Redwood Road, which would later become his prune and apple farm. Hill worked for Louis Wurz Sr. for 16 years on his ranches, later becoming a partner to Al and Louis Wurz Jr. Hill bought his own farm in 1957, on Redwood Road, just west of Browns Valley Road. A total of 36.5 acres were in prunes, and 12 acres were in apples. Hill irrigated his apple orchards by pumping from the nearby Redwood Creek. (Courtesy Joseph Hill.)

JOE HILL AND HENRY PADRONE WORKING ON THE HILL APPLE FARM ON REDWOOD ROAD, 1962. In 1959, the *Napa County Record* reported that Hill "sells 6,000 boxes of apples a year from his orchard . . . He is the best known and largest producer of apples in this area." Dubbed the "Apple King," Hill cultivated many varieties including: Red & Golden Delicious, Jonathan, Red June, Astrachan, Pippin, Roman Beauty, Winter Banana, Spitzenberg (now almost entirely grafted over to Red Delicious). The Apple King later added a new planting of one acre of the recent original variety of the Crimson Red Delicious. (Courtesy Joseph Hill.)

DeHaven Prunes and Pears. Before its development, this area was planted with 15 acres of prunes and pears, along with 20 acres of vineyards and pastures. The DeHavens had their fruit picked and processed in a dehydrator built in 1935. (Courtesy Dr. Jim Atwood.)

View of DeHaven Land in 1968. The DeHaven ranch was photographed a few months before the land was cleared for development. The Rancho de Napa Mobile Home Park in Yountville was constructed on property once owned by the DeHaven family. (Courtesy Dr. Jim Atwood.)

IVY LOEBER. Loeber's grandfather Calvin Griffith arrived in the Napa Valley in 1845, when it was still Mexican territory. Ivy Loeber was a leader in the effort to make Calistoga's Bale Mill a state park. In 1974 it was conveyed to the California State Park System for preservation and eventual restoration. Ivy Loeber: "As Father Serra traveled he scattered to the right, and to the left, the mustard seeds which he had brought with him from Spain. The following year, as they returned south they followed 'a ribbon of gold' . . . So wherever you see the Spanish mustard in California you know the Spanish fathers visited there. This is the early California legend as told to me by my grandfather, whose father told it to him." (Courtesy Napa County Historical Society.)

SIMPKINS DAIRY, 1971. Cliff Simpkins is pictured with son Brad and daughter Claire. Cliff's uncle, Tommy Simpkins, had a dairy on Foster Road that offered home delivery. Paula Amen Judah remembers, "Our family's milk was delivered in glass bottles—my mom would pour off the rich cream, which rose to the top, to use in her morning coffee. The milkman would also bring cottage cheese or eggs, if we left a note asking for it." (Courtesy Clifford Simpkins.)

SIMPKINS DAIRY RANCH, NORTH AND SECOND AVENUES, 1971. Brad Simpkins is pictured with a calf at Grandparents Alfred L. and Rachel A (Gimple) Simpkins's farm on Second Avenue. John Clift Simpkins and Eva Burnell Simpkins purchased the land in 1886 from Napa City founder, Nathan Coombs. Six generations of Simpkins have continuously lived on the property since then. (Courtesy Clifford Simpkins.)

BRAD SIMPKINS MILKING COW, 1971. Sister Claire waits her turn at the family dairy farm. Other area dairies included Hill Brook at Third Avenue North, Lewis Dairy on Coombsville Road, Dante Fomazi in Browns Valley, Bobby Fomazi at Staggs Leap, Ray Luiz in Rutherford, Swizick's on Silverado Trail, Cabal Brothers in Carneros, Stewarts on Highway 29 south of Napa, Walt Crivelli on Old Sonoma Highway, Ed Tomani in Calistoga, Dr. Parrot on Big Ranch Road, Pridmore Dairy in Berryessa, and Stornetta's Dairy. (Courtesy Cliff Simpkins.)

CORN HARVESTING. Here, corn is being harvested near Howell Mountain Road in the late 1970s. (Courtesy Pacific Union College).

OLD AGRICULTURE BUILDING CLASSROOM, PACIFIC UNION COLLEGE, C. 1975. Pacific Union College treasures its agricultural heritage: "Through all of its Angwin years the College has tilled a number of plots of land and make us of the fruits thereof." (Courtesy Pacific Union College.)

WOMAN MILKING COW AT THE PACIFIC UNION COLLEGE IN ANGWIN. In 1977, Kay Archuleta wrote, "Who will ever forget the lush green pastures with their black and white and red and white and fawn colored cows?" (Courtesy Pacific Union College.)

GRANDE/ROSSI BARN ON SILVERADO TRAIL, OCTOBER 1979. Dorothy Rossi was born on the Rossi farm 90 years ago and has lived her whole life on the ranch in the original home next to the barn. (Courtesy Dorothy Rossi.)

GRANDE/ROSSI RANCH ON SILVERADO TRAIL, 1979. Dorothy Rossi's son also lives on the property and cares for the vineyards and orchards. Their ranch is across the street from John and Margaret Hoffman's walnut orchards featured in chapter six. (Courtesy Dorothy Rossi.)

GUIDUCCI RANCH, AUGUST 1981. The family ranch was built by James's great-grandfather Carlo Brignoli, who emigrated from northern Italy after the turn of the century. East Napa, the neighborhood that had been Juarez's Tulocay Grant, became Napa's "Little Italy." Italian houses all had two kitchens, one in the basement and one on the first floor, in case of flooding. (Courtesy James Guiducci.)

GUIDUCCI WAGON. Jason Guiducci takes a break in an empty prune box on August 1981: "When the boxes were stacked too high, you had a full load of prunes (around two tons)." (Courtesy James Guiducci.)

GUIDUCCI FAMILY PICKING PRUNES. Pictured from left to right are grandfather Moe Ocskay, father Jim, Jason Guiducci, and dog Burlin. James remembers, "It was one of the last operable prune orchards in the valley still selling to Sunsweet until 1987. Each August, my family would converge on the farm to help pick prunes. My cousins, aunts, and uncles would visit from out of town to help." (Courtesy James Guiducci.)

GUIDUCCI RANCH, 1981. Moe Ocskay is shaking trees, and Jason and James Guiducci are on the tractor. James Guiducci remembers, "The fields were plowed by a late 1930s model tractor, which ran until 1987 when the last crop was harvested at my grandfather's ranch . . . In the past 10 years, my grandfather has had his drinking-water well redrilled three times in order to find freshwater deeper. No doubt the vast acres of the new surrounding vineyards have put intense pressure on the finite aquifer." (Courtesy James Guiducci.)

JOSE NAVARRO AND DAUGHTER RAQUEL AT 1704 SPENCER STREET, 1987.
Farmer Nathan Fay, who developed some of Napa's earliest prize-winning wines, hired Jose Navarro in August 1975, to harvest grapes. In July 1980, Jose brought his family—wife Lilia and daughters Maria and Raquel—from Mexico. Mr. Fay offered him a fulltime job as a foreman. In 1982, Fay provided the Navarros a house on Spencer Street to live rent-free. When Nathan Fay retired in 1985, he wanted to make sure the family had housing security and so deeded the house to Jose Navarro. This act of generosity enabled the family to buy Jefferson Food Market, which they owned from 2000 to 2006. (Courtesy Lilia Navarro.)

LILIA NAVARRO WITH DAUGHTER RAQUEL, 1987. The Mexican community in Napa increased as orchards were converted to vineyards, offering employment opportunities. In 1985, Lilia Navarra began teaching Ballet Folklorico Mexican dances. She remembers, "Everybody learned and danced together—Mexican and Anglo kids. Girls and boys were very excited and happy . . . Those were for me unforgettable days." Raquel was the first American-born generation of her family to graduate from college, at UCLA. (Courtesy Lilia Navarro.)

DAVID ELLSWORTH ON VICHY AVENUE, 1987. The six pear trees here had been planted on the property by the previous owner. "These trees were the backdrop to our lives," says his mother, Mary Ann. Paula Amen Judah remembers driving through east Napa when she was about the same age as David: "We'd all pile into our roomy blue Frazier. My father would drive up Hoffman Avenue, turn right, past the cemetery, and head out Coombsville Road toward Mt. George, where my sister and I began the ritual of counting cows, soothed by the flow of acreage as we passed." (Courtesy Mary Ann Ellsworth.)

FATHER AND SON ON PORCH AT SPENCER STREET. María Navarro, daughter of José and Lilia, married Jorge Esparza at the family home in 1987. Pictured are her husband, Jorge, on the porch with their son Jorge Jr. in 1990. (Courtesy Lilia Navarro.)

PHONG AND CUONG VU, 1984. Dr. Phong Vu writes, "When we first came here to Napa from Vietnam, my father found a temporary job working on the Napa College campus. . . . For several years I remember my mother taking my brother and me to the pear orchards. At first, because I was so young, my mother would tell me to wait on the concrete while she and my brother would go pick the trees. She would tell me that there were snakes nearby, which I guess scared me enough to stay put . . . Then as I got a little bit older she eventually had me help out. We'd come fully prepared with our brown paper grocery bags and just pick away, sometimes until daylight was gone." (Courtesy Phong Vu.)

KATHRYN AND MICHAEL HAVENS. The Havens tasting the juice of their first commercial wine in 1984. They began production at Cassayre-Forni Cellars on Manley Lane (Mike Forni is on the press in the background) before moving operations, first to Eighth Street in Napa, and then to Hoffman Lane in Yountville. (Courtesy Kathryn and Michael Havens.)

TIFFANY AND BRANDON, HILL GRANDCHILDREN ON TRACTOR IN NAPA, 1987. When Joe Hill sold his Redwood Road ranch in the early 1980s, he bought acreage on Galleron Road in St. Helena. (Courtesy Joseph Hill.)

Six

The Persistence of Pollen

1990–2010

Pear Bread
by Peggy Aaron

3 cups flour
1 teaspoon baking soda
¼ teaspoon baking power
1 teaspoon salt
1½ teaspoon cinnamon
3 eggs slightly beaten
¾ cup vegetable oil (I use canola)
2 cups sugar
2 cups peeled and chopped pears
2 teaspoons vanilla extract
1 cup chopped walnuts

Preheat oven to 325 degrees.
Grease and flour two 8½-inch x 4½-inch loaf pans.
Combine flour, baking soda, baking powder, salt, and cinnamon in a medium bowl.
Mix eggs, oil, sugar, pears, and vanilla in a small bowl.
Add to flour mixture, stirring just until moistened. Stir in nuts if using.
Spoon into pans.
Bake 1 hour, 10 minutes until a wooden pick inserted in center comes out clean.
Cool 10 minutes before removing from pans. Slice when cool.
Makes two loaves.
Very moist, freezes well in freezer bag or wrapped in foil.

FIG TREE, CONNOLLY RANCH. Pictured here is Lauren Ellsworth at the ranch where 3,000 children each year attend workshops like Farm Animal Tour, Early Pioneer Life, and Dirt to Dine. (Courtesy Lauren Coodley.)

ESPALIERED APPLE TREE AT CONNOLLY RANCH. Lynne Andresen is one of Napa's master gardeners who tends these trees. (Courtesy Lynne Andresen.)

CHILD VISITING CONNOLLY RANCH. Harold Kelly recounts, "When I got to know Peggy Connolly, I enjoyed listening to her as she spoke of how much pleasure she got from watching children feed her animals. She told me she would like to see children continue to learn about farm life, and left her property to The Land Trust, telling me, 'Do what is right.' She died a few months later [in 1991]." (Courtesy Oscar Vega.)

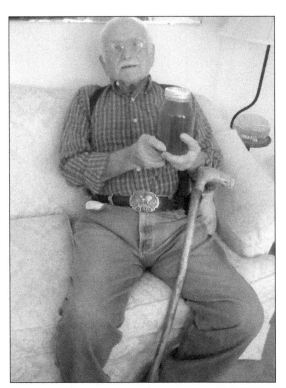

BEEKEEPER SWEDE JOHNSON. For 40 years, Swede has raised bees and made honey. He always wanted to be a baker and a cook, but growing up in the Depression made that impossible. He worked as a boilermaker for 35 years at Basalt. Swede began beekeeping at Spencer and E Streets, where has lived for 30 years and kept up to 12 hives. In addition to raising bees, he bakes his own bread every day and cans many kinds of produce. He has not needed allergy treatment since the 1960s, which he attributes to his regular consumption of local honey (Courtesy Lauren Coodley.)

ETHEL WESSMAN PICKING OLIVES. The 90-year-old mother of Kathryn Havens harvests Manzanilla olives from trees planted by the Havens at their Hoffman Lane property. The olives were processed for eating, rather than oil. (Courtesy Kathryn and Michael Havens.)

112

LAUREN ELLSWORTH'S FOURTH BIRTHDAY, 1990. Lauren and friends celebrate under the shade of the pear trees, which were bearing fruit that summer. In attendance was her grandmother Victoria Ellsworth, who canned pears and peaches and baked pies for her family. (Courtesy Mary Ann Ellsworth.)

QUINCE TREE AT CONNOLLY RANCH. This is one of the very few quince trees left in Napa. Former city council member Harold Kelly remembers, "Sometime in sixties, the Connolly sisters moved fulltime to the ranch when they retired from their careers in San Francisco. I was active in the Browns Valley Area; Helen got involved with the neighborhood association. Along with me, they were among the original signers of Measure J." Passed in 1990, Measure J was a Napa County general plan amendment that sought to preserve all agriculturally designated land. (Courtesy Lauren Coodley.)

ASIAN PEARS. This fruit comes from an Asian pear orchard, planted by a Korean farmer around 1980, the only one left in Napa County. The Carneros area was known for its apricots, apples, peaches, and plums. In the late 19th century, Francis Cutting owned 400 acres of orchards there. He shipped about 1,600 tons of fruit from Cuttings Wharf to San Francisco. (Courtesy Dona Bonick.)

BONICK ORCHARD. John, Dona, and son Max Bonick found the two acres of Asian pear trees on their property in Carneros. Now they are organic farmers who sell at a roadside stand and to restaurants. (Courtesy Dona Bonick.)

114

LEXA MALINAK PICKING APRICOTS, 2006.
Lexa enjoys her first time harvesting apricots at Groggy and Pop Pop's home (grandparents Lynn and Ron Ford). Lynn writes, "When we moved to Napa we were told that Napa was not a good place to grow apricots and were advised to cut the old tree down. Needless to say we were overjoyed when this little tree worked so hard and gave us such a bountiful crop." (Courtesy Lynn Ford.)

CONNOLLY RANCH GRAVENSTEIN APPLE TREE. Educational director Michael Lauher stands with one of the oldest trees at the Connolly Ranch. Michael began working at Connolly with his family as a volunteer in 2002; in 2003, he was hired as a full-time employee for the ranch. (Courtesy Lauren Coodley.)

CHICKENS, WOMBATS' FARM. Chicken owner Áine Kelly says, "Chickens can make great pets as well as great eggs." This chicken is named Blanca. (Courtesy Lauren Coodley.)

KEIJI SUGIYAMA BESIDE HIS FUJI APPLE TREE. His parents knew Juzo Hamamoto, who ran an apple dryer near the RMS Brandy distillery in Los Carneros: "He had relatives in Penngrove where we lived. When we were little kids, we used to come visit them in the late thirties and early forties. He used to give us apples because, you know, we were his friends." Mr Hamamoto's business never recovered after internment: "I was about 12 years old and we were first sent to Merced, along with the family of Mr Hamamoto. Then we were sent to a camp in Colorado. We'd see the barbed wire but . . . you know . . . we were only 12." After Juzo Hamamoto was released from internment camp, his drying business had been sold off, but he still operated an apple stand on Los Carneros Drive. Keiji Sugiyama was hired at Silverado Middle School in 1959 to teach metal shop and math, and he later taught metal shop at Vintage until his retirement in 1992. He has been growing fruit trees at his home since 1966. (Courtesy Haley Rekdahl.)

ANITA CATLIN. Catlin is holding a jar of her plum jam at her ranch at Pope Valley, located on the Locallomi land grant, given to Julian and Juliana Pope by Mariano Vallejo for 25¢. (Courtesy Lauren Coodley.)

SONITA OLIVER PICKING BLACKBERRIES. Blackberries grow wild all over the valley. Anita Catlin explains, "We take the truck down with lug boxes and cut big branches full of blackberries along the creek bed. We all have purple fingers and clothes. We sort them in the kitchen. To make syrup you boil them with sugar, and strain, for jam you don't need to strain. At the Catlin Farm, berrying occurs around the Fourth of July." (Courtesy Lynn Ford.)

SERGIO MARTINEZ HARVESTING CORN. "Trefethen Family Vineyards is a working farm," says Jon Ruel, Trefethen's director of viticulture and winemaking, "so we decided to put that theme into practice to benefit our employees." In 2006, Jon and one of his vineyard crews began planting vegetables on a half-acre fallow field on the estate and named it La Huerta, or "small vegetable farm." Fruits, nuts, and a wide variety of herbs are also grown in the five acres surrounding the historic villa. (Courtesy Trefethen Winery.)

MULTIPLE VEGETABLES AT LA HUERTA. All Trefethen employees partake of this bounty, which they either pick up at the orchard or have delivered to their departments. Summer of 2010, the orchard yielded 500 pounds of sweet corn, 250 pounds of onions, 200 pounds of apples and "more blackberries than you can shake a vole at." Jon jokes, "Maybe one day we'll change our name to Trefethen Family Farms and be as well-known for our produce as our wine!" (Courtesy Trefethen Winery.)

VOLUNTEERS, BRAIN FOOD GARDEN, YOUNTVILLE. The Tug McGraw Foundation has created a 40-foot-square "Brain Food Garden" that will produce fruits, vegetables and herbs that have been shown to help the human brain function and recover from injuries. Jennifer Brusstar writes, "The woman is Billie Hewitt who is a member of the Napa County Master Gardeners and shares a passion for growing food year-round. Billie helped us put our garden together to help teach others the simplicity of eating delicious and eating local . . . She owns Your Edible Garden. The man is Frank Henderson, Board member and Tug McGraw's cousin. He is retired and gives his time to what we call the grunt and coordination efforts of our garden." (Courtesy Tug McGraw Foundation.)

CHILDREN VISITING BRAIN FOOD GARDEN. Pictured from left to right are Grace Vlandis, Eli Souza, Clarice Rivera, and Dustin Huntzinger. (Courtesy Tug McGraw Foundation.)

CAROLE AND KENI KENT WITH OLIVE
TREES ON THEIR WOMBATS' FARM.
"The experience of watching olive trees
move from flower to fruit, and
getting from that fruit a delicious oil
is indescribable . . . We're trying to
farm in a way that rejuvenates and
does not simply exploit the soil."
(Courtesy Lauren Coodley.)

KENI KENT AND HIS BEEHIVES. "Bees are so crucial to pollination, and their survival is threatened. Raising bees is a service to oneself, to one's own crops and then to the larger community." (Courtesy Lauren Coodley.)

JACK TOGNETTI, OWNER AND GROWER, ALOISE FRANCISCO VINEYARDS, 2011. Standing tall and in charge at age 94, Jack Tognetti takes a short break from his spring pruning. Before retiring from American President Lines in 1973, Jack and wife Camille bought the ranch on Bayview Avenue in the Carneros region of Napa. At the time of purchase, walnut, pear, and prune orchards covered the property, along with persimmon, plum, apple, fig, and peach trees. After retiring, Jack began remodeling the little house there, which became the Tognettis' permanent residence: "I added a nice kitchen, and for a couple of years I sold pears and prunes to Mrs. von Uhlit, and she resold them. We sometimes took our prunes to the Sunrise Dryer in Fairfield . . . we were barely able to pay our taxes with the proceeds." In 1975, Jack began to take out the pears and prunes and replant with wine grapes. He had converted 15 acres to vineyard by 1980, and he kept five acres in walnut. The walnuts from his 100-year-old trees quickly sell out each season. Tognetti raises award-winning camellias as well, but he is most known for the superb Chardonnay grapes his vineyards produce.

SUNSWEET BUILDING. In 1977, Louis Ezettie wrote, "Every year we kids earned enough money picking prunes at the Frank Bush Ranch near Little Trancas to pay for school clothes and school books . . . Once one of the great prune growing areas in the state, Napa County had seen the industry give way to an almost complete turnover to grape growing. Sunsweet disposed of the packing and shipping departments on Jackson Street, and reduced their workforce from 100 to 25 people." (Courtesy Lauren Coodley.)

GEORGE TANITA'S LAST PRUNE TREE. As kids, George and his brothers spent summers helping with the harvest. This 50-year-old-prune tree is the lone survivor on the Tanita Ranch on Big Ranch Road, where the family once had 60 acres of prune and walnut orchards. Eikichi and Kusu Tanita bought the property in the early 1930s. Grandson George strives to keep the tree alive, which still produces every year. His dog Tike, a prune lover, devours all the fruit from the bottom limbs. (Courtesy George Tanita.)

JOHN AND MARGARET HOFFMAN. The couple, married 70 years, pause for a photograph while visiting with a family of walnut pickers late in the season of 2009, John's last walnut harvest. Before converting most of their prune orchards to walnut, the Hoffman's sold their prune crop to the Sunsweet plant on Jackson Street. After a hot day of picking, the whole family would go swimming in the Napa River behind their farm. The grafted walnut trees, which now dominate the farm, John planted from seed. (Courtesy Laure Latham.)

WALNUTS DRYING. John Hoffman dries walnuts on wood trays according to ancestral techniques In addition to three varieties of walnuts, his organic farm boasts three kinds of prunes and plums, 20 kinds of apples (including Arkansas Black, Hoffman's favorite), and four kinds of persimmons. The farm also has loquat, jujube, peach, mulberry, apricot, and fig, plus olallieberry and boysenberry vines. Beehives within the orchards assure pollination. (Courtesy Laure Latham.)

JOHN HOFFMAN WITH HIS CUSTOM DRYING TRAYS. Horticulturist, educator, arborist, and author John Hoffman is pictured at age 93, hosting visitors to his U-Pick farm. When the Hoffmans bought the 23 acres in 1949, it was planted mostly in French prunes, along with about three-quarters of an acre of Bartlett pears and an acre of cherries. Called "Brother John of the Trees" by his master gardener colleagues, Hoffman died on May 26, 2010. (Courtesy Laure Latham.)

SIGN ON SILVERADO TRAIL. John and Margaret Hoffman joined the Napa County Farming Trails and hung its sign next to their mailbox at 2125 Silverado Trail. The sign remains today, though, one by one, small farms disappeared, until the Hoffmans were the only members. Below the Farming Trail logo, the Hoffmans would hang a notice of what produce was in season: pears in August, walnuts in September and October, persimmons in December, and for one weekend each year, quince. (Courtesy Laure Latham.)

BIBLIOGRAPHY

Ahmann, Judy Ann, editor. *Some California Ranches—Their Stories and Their Brands*. California Cattle Women, 2010.

Alexander, Pat. Images of America: *Yountville*. Charleston, SC: Arcadia Publishing, 2009.

Archuleta, Kay. *The Brannan Saga*. Illuminations Press, 1977.

Butler, W.D. "The Cherry Industry of Napa County." *Bulletin of the Department of Agriculture, State of California, 1917*.

Chappell, Violet Parrish and Vivian Parrish Wilder. "Pomo Elders Speak." *The Sonoma County Gazette Newspaper* Volume 7, Number 10, October 1–November 4, 2010.

Coodley, Lauren and Paula Amen Schmitt. *If Not to History: Recovering the Stories of Women in Napa*. Napa County Historical Society, 2009.

Coodley, Lauren, with Paula Amen Schmitt. *Napa: The Transformation of an American Town*. Charleston, SC: Arcadia Publishing, 2007.

Couchman, Robert. *The Sunsweet Story*. San Jose: Sunsweet Growers Inc., 1967.

Duhig, Stewart M. *Huichica*. Napa: Viola Duhig, 1990.

Hoffman, John. *Trees of Napa Valley*. University of California Cooperative Extension & Master Gardeners of Napa County, 2002).

Le Guin, Ursula K. *Always Coming Home*. University of California Press, 2001. (Used by permission of the author and the author's agents, the Virginia Kidd Agency, Inc.)

Menefee, C.A. *Historical Descriptive Sketch Book of Napa, Sonoma, Lake and Mendocino Counties*. Napa: Reporter Publishing Co., 1873.

Napa Register articles by Rebecca Yerger, Natalie Hoffman, Gary Brady-Herndon, Frances Proctor, Kerana Todorov, Marsha Dorgan, Louis Ezettie.

Native American Garden: A Guide to Plants and Their Uses. Bothe State Park, Calistoga. Out of print.

Street, Richard Steven. *Beasts of the Field: A Narrative History of California Farmworkers, 1769–1913*. Stanford University Press, 2004.

Visit us at
arcadiapublishing.com

Ingram Content Group UK Ltd.
Milton Keynes UK
UKHW032007260523
422432UK00010B/90

9 781531 649661